THOMAS CROMWELL

and
The English Reformation

A. G. DICKENS

HODDER AND STOUGHTON
LONDON   SYDNEY   AUCKLAND   TORONTO

ISBN 0 340 21283 7

First published 1959; sixth impression 1977

Printed in Great Britain for Hodder & Stoughton Educational, a
division of Hodder & Stoughton Ltd., Mill Road, Dunton Green,
Sevenoaks, Kent by J. W. Arrowsmith Ltd., Bristol

Contents

Acknowledgments

I GRATEFULLY acknowledge advice on many important points from Dr. A. L. Rowse. Professors G. R. Elton and G. W. O. Woodward both gave much unselfish assistance with a variety of knotty problems, while Professor G. R. Potter at a crucial stage provided a rousing private tutorial on the Reformation. Many years before writing this book, I felt the need for a succinct provisional reassessment of Thomas Cromwell, yet I am glad I did not attempt one until after the appearance of Geoffrey Elton's stimulating researches. Again, in framing Chapter VII, I made very extensive use of Dr. J. F. Mozley's *Coverdale and his Bibles* and, while operating in the field of political ideas, certain chapters of Professor W. G. Zeeveld's *Foundations of Tudor Policy* were seldom far from my thoughts. Though my conclusions often differ radically from those of R. B. Merriman, I could not avoid incurring a deep obligation to his labours, especially in matters concerning Cromwell's early life and foreign policy.

Numerous books and articles on the period have appeared since this book was originally published. They have demanded few actual corrections, yet they supplement many of my themes and I have accordingly rewritten the Select Bibliography for a second time.

Institute of Historical Research, 1976.

Chapter One

Early Life

BETWEEN the fall of Wolsey and the hapless last years of Henry VIII, there came to power an administrator of tremendous energy, an institutional thinker, a patron of political philosophers, a bold and original statesman who thought of his own work as creative and who cast his shadow centuries forward upon the history of England. No major figure of that history has suffered from so many misconceptions and calumnies as Thomas Cromwell. Some aspects of the tenacious black legend were invited by his real shortcomings; more still arose from the uncritical acceptance of information supplied by his bitterest enemies; yet most derived from those Victorian ecclesiastical animosities, liberal anachronisms and genteel prejudices which even now encumber our thinking and influence our choices within the Tudor world. Of Cromwell's first thirty-five years we know relatively little, yet that little possesses great significance, for it prepares us to witness the advent of a new man to the controls of the State, a man largely emancipated from those ecclesiastical and neo-feudal values which still held the custom-ridden bulk of English society in their grasp.

Thomas Cromwell was born about the year of Bosworth: though not quite a Londoner by birth, he must have been familiar from early years with the many-spired but malodorous city in and around which his years of greatness were to be passed. By a fortunate survival, the court-rolls of the manor of Wimbledon have preserved several facts concerning his family background. His father Walter pursued various business concerns at Putney; brewer, blacksmith and fuller, he also contrived to lead a life of somewhat more than average turbulence. Though apparently related to the rich Nottinghamshire magnate Ralph Lord Cromwell, he inherited few graces. In 1477 he paid a fine for assaulting and drawing blood; he was frequently amerced for drunkenness, for overburdening the common with his cattle, for cutting more than his share of the furze and thorns, and—a normal professional hazard—for selling ale without inspection by the ale-taster. In 1480 he held two virgates of land in Putney and in 1500 received six more by grant from Archbishop Morton. He became a constable of Putney in 1495 and served frequently as a juror. He last appears in 1514, when he had encountered serious trouble, the lord of the manor having evicted him from his copyholds, because he had 'falsely and fraudulently erased the evidences and terrures of the lord to the perturbation and disturbance of the lord and his tenants'. The elder of Walter's two recorded daughters married a substantial Welshman and became mother of Richard Williams, who was knighted, took the name of Cromwell, and is remembered as great-grandfather of Protector Oliver. The younger daughter married a sheepfarmer euphoniously named Wellyfed; their son was ultimately brought up with his cousin Gregory, son of Thomas Cromwell.

As for Thomas himself, he left home under less happy auspices than his sisters. Unlike his friend Latimer, who was born in no higher degree, he never looked back with pride upon his early life or went to the trouble of recording its details. We are thus dependent upon a number of unverifiable or unsatisfactory anecdotes in Foxe's *Acts and Monuments*, upon a short story based on Cromwell's life by the Italian novelist Bandello, and upon some brief reports from his bitter enemies Cardinal Pole and the Imperial ambassador Chapuys. Foxe asserts that Cromwell told Archbishop Cranmer 'what a ruffian he was in his younger days', a remark probably not intended in the self-condemnatory sense assumed by humourless modern critics. He was certainly brought up in a rough school. Pole relates that he became a roving soldier in Italy, and Bandello that he served with the French army at the Battle of the Garigliano in December 1503. Arriving penniless in Florence and sensing a lack of future in the military life, he entered the service of the rich banker Frescobaldo and also worked as an accountant for a Venetian firm. After two years or more of business-life in northern Italy, it may have been at Pisa that he met some English merchants, who persuaded him to join them in the Netherlands. Here, writes Pole, he spent several years as a business consultant, making local reports to the London merchants on the state of trade throughout the Netherlands.

Foxe's story concerning Cromwell's second visit to Italy was derived from the martyrologist's native town of Boston, and despite its novelish detail, it may form one of the more authentic elements in the early biography. The townsmen of Boston sent to Rome a certain Geoffrey Chambers—he figures in later life as one of Cromwell's agents—in order to obtain the renewal of certain pardons. Chambers doubted his own capabilities and, passing through Antwerp, persuaded Cromwell to accompany him to Rome. Desirous of saving time and money, and knowing how Pope Julius liked strange delicacies, Cromwell prepared certain dishes of jelly in the English fashion, hitherto unknown in Rome. Choosing a moment when the pontiff had just returned from hunting, Cromwell brought in the dishes 'with a three man's song, as we call it in the English tongue'. The Pope, marvelling at the strangeness of the music, called them into his presence. With a caution appropriate to the place and period, he commanded a cardinal to try the jelly, then partook himself and ended by sealing the Boston pardons on the spot. Here at least is one of the anecdotes which one most desires to believe, for it seems so completely in character: it displays the Cromwellian directness, the timing, the economy of means and the touch of sardonic humour. This journey is assigned to the year 1510 and Cromwell must soon have returned to the Netherlands trade, since the letter of an English mercer written many years afterwards recalls a favour Cromwell had done in connection with the cloth mart at Middleburgh in 1512. The state-papers also contain suggestions that he was living both in the Netherlands and in England during this same year, which is taken to be the date of his marriage and resettlement in England.

Though we enjoy few reliable glimpses of his *Wanderjahre*, Cromwell's mature character and public policies both testify abundantly to the educational effects of this period. An Englishman could never entirely return to his native simplicities after having spent two years or more in Italy at the time when Cesare Borgia was exhibiting *virtù*, when Machiavelli was learning the ruses of diplomacy, when Raphael was painting, and when, at the court of Urbino, those famed evening conversations were furnishing material for the *Book of the Courtier*. High Renaissance Italy still maintained her poise; she was not yet resigned to expiating her individualism under the whips of foreign oppressors and clad in the penitential garb of the Counter Reformation. Here the facts still tended to outrun the imaginations of modern poets and novelists; here Browning's insidious Duke had his innumerable counterparts in real life. Italian society had devoted itself to aesthetic rather than to moral ideals; it could boast man's highest artistic and intellectual achievements since the decline of Greece, and yet inevitably it had left educated men to spend too much of their lives on the dark side of the moon. It was a society compounded of high aspirations and sordid realities, both of them alternating rapidly in the life of the individual. Too often the afternoon's elegiacs were succeeded by the dagger-thrust in the dark *piazza*. Climate and temperament, the proximity of the cultured infidel, the involved state-system, the corroding temptations of the papal court, the rediscovery of the antique, the enervating breath of ancient grandeurs and corruptions: all these had long made Italy a unique world, one in which many a dazzled barbarian had reeled with horror and delight on descending the mountain barriers from the north.

Its emancipatory effect upon the Italianate Englishman was already greeted with distrust by conservative English society. Just as today a year in America often liberates an Englishman from the more cloying reverences of European Social Democracy, so a period in Renaissance Italy then liberated his predecessor from both the superstitions and the pieties of a priest-dominated and scholastic-minded society north of the Alps. It did not necessarily produce an immoralism, still less an agnosticism, but rather a certain radical detachment, a trick of thinking in terms of efficiency and effectiveness, an ability to abstract problems (whether of physical science or of the State) from their hitherto accepted theological or teleological context, and to submit them to a cold and factual analysis. It helped a man to see through himself and not to rationalize his own misdeeds with that pathetic pseudo-religious cant and self-deception which marked barbarian rulers and politicians. It helped him to avoid acting in hot blood, to dissimulate his passions, to reject unduly rigid systems of ideas, to realize the truth of Guicciardini's words: 'it is a great mistake to talk of things of the world absolutely, without discriminating, and as it were by rule. For in nearly everything there are distinctions and exceptions, due to variety of circumstances. These circumstances you cannot treat by one and the same standard. They are not to be found in books. You must learn them from your own discretion.'

Above all, Italy helped a man to see his northern world with new eyes and, if he aspired to govern its affairs, to propound fresh answers free of hidebound tradition. We shall in due course review the controversy as to whether Cromwell actually took Machiavelli's *Prince* as his textbook, yet the question can claim little more than antiquarian interest. A man who had travelled extensively and worked in Machiavelli's Italy had little to learn from his book, which was scarcely more Machiavellian than the common political practice and conversation of the day. If we saw a business man with years of experience in America introducing American notions into a European firm, we should not attribute his action to some fashionable textbook from the Harvard School of Business Administration.

The spectacle of the young Cromwell working in the Netherlands has an interest equal to that of his Italian experiences. No training-ground could have been more profitable for a future English statesman than the marts and bourse of Antwerp, the greatest commercial capital the world had hitherto seen. It was a uniquely cosmopolitan city, containing large and permanent colonies of businessmen from all the trading nations of Europe. It was the funnel through which English wool and cloth passed to half the Continent, and through which the Portuguese, with their monopoly of the oriental spice-trade, distributed their vital commodity to the unrefrigerated storehouses and larders of the western world. It was soon to become by far the chief money-market of Europe. As an eminent Manchester scholar has written: 'Antwerp was not only the London but the Manchester of the sixteenth century.'

At this time the Merchant Adventurers, backed by the government, were still waging an economic struggle of the first importance to this country: the struggle to convert the export of wool and unfinished cloth into that of the finished article, hence to derive the maximum profit from our resources, while yet creating employment in England. His participation in these affairs brought Cromwell to the heart of our economic problems, which, as the Netherlands fell under unsympathetic Spanish rule and England nevertheless became dependent on the Antwerp money-market, were destined to increase in complexity. When he came to high office, Cromwell naturally showed a most expert grasp of these all-important relationships, and the one other Tudor statesman who can compare with him in this field had likewise received his training in Antwerp. Beside Cromwell and

Sir Thomas Gresham, the products of English country-house and academic life cut many an amateurish caper when they tried to organize the nation's trade and finance.

About 1512 Cromwell made an advantageous match with Elizabeth Wykys, a woman of more refined background than his own. She came of an old family of gentry and, though her father was in the wool trade, her uncle had been gentleman-usher to Henry VII. Romantic marriages were almost unknown in the circles to which she and Cromwell belonged, and Elizabeth seems to have brought him some useful money. Chapuys disparages Cromwell's wife as the daughter of a shearman, but adds the more significant fact that for some time after his marriage Cromwell kept servants in his house to continue the business of his father-in-law. The point finds corroboration in Cromwell's own correspondence, which shows that in 1524, years after he had turned to a legal and official career, he was still trading in cloth and wool. Of his family life we know little, but none of his enemies ever hinted that his morality in this sphere was other than exemplary, either before or after the early death of his wife. His heir, the dull and modest Gregory, was born in 1513, and there followed two daughters, Anne and Grace. In 1525 appears his only surviving letter to his wife, written during a visit to Kent. It is the letter from any Tudor businessman or landowner to his spouse: amiable, partnerly, but with its eye firmly on business matters. 'To my well beloved wife Elizabeth Cromwell against the Friars Augustines in London be this given. Elizabeth, I commend me unto you and have sent by this bearer a fat doe, the one half whereof, I pray you, may be delivered unto my gossip mistress Smyth, and with the rest to use at your pleasure. And further if Richard Swifte be come home or fortune to come shortly, I will that he resort to me at Begham or Tonbridge with all diligence. Such news as you have in those parts I pray you send me part by this bearer. At Begham the 29th day of November. And farther, I pray you send me word in writing who hath resorted unto you since my departure from you, to speak with me. Per your husband, Thomas Cromwell.' Within three years or so Elizabeth had died; perhaps she succumbed to the sweating sickness which ravaged the country in the years 1527–8. At all events, in the will Cromwell wrote in July 1529 she is 'my late wife'. At this time his mother-in-law Mercy Priour was apparently keeping house for him, since it is for her that he then makes elaborate and affectionate provision, including the bequest of much household stuff.

Meantime Cromwell's life had been gradually moving into new paths, though a curious lack of trustworthy records between 1512 and 1520 leaves some important biographical problems unsolved. During these years there occurred in London a violent crisis between clergy and laity, and thence between Church and State. The case of Richard Hunne and its aftermath form in retrospect an important prelude to the crisis of the Reformation Parliament, and it would not be unduly bold to hazard a guess regarding Cromwell's personal sympathies. Hunne was a substantial merchant tailor, but refused on principle to surrender the bearing-cloth which his parish priest claimed, by way of the usual mortuary dues, on the death of Hunne's baby. The priest prosecuted him in the Bishop's consistory court and won, whereupon Hunne foolishly and unsuccessfully brought him into the King's Bench to answer a *praemunire* charge. The churchmen responded by arresting Hunne for heresy and a search of his house yielded some heretical books, including a Wycliffite bible. After examination by Bishop Fitzjames, an unpopular prelate regarded by Erasmus as the worst type of reactionary, Hunne was returned to the Lollards' Tower at St. Paul's.

This took place on Saturday, 2 December 1514, and on the following Monday morning he was found with his neck broken. After an investigation of the cell, the body and various witnesses, a jury found a verdict of wilful murder against the Bishop's Chancellor Dr. Horsey and two of his henchmen. Readers interested to unravel the complex detective-aspects of this crime should begin with Mr. Ogle's book *The Tragedy of the Lollards' Tower*, since Gairdner and other earlier historians strain every probability and wilfully neglect much evidence in order to exculpate Horsey. In fact, as Mr. Ogle has conclusively shown, his guilt may be regarded as all but certain. Bishop Fitzjames did not, however, show any lack of confidence; he pronounced Hunne a heretic, handed over his body to be burned at Smithfield and thereby reduced his wife and children to pauperism. All London was aflame, and when Parliament met in January 1515 it sought to renew an Act of 1513, which stripped benefit of clergy from the troublesome host of clerics in minor orders. There followed a series of disputes between the bishops on the one hand and the King's Franciscan chaplain Dr. Standish, supported by the judges, on the other. The bishops made no secret of their desire to charge Standish with heresy and he ostentatiously appealed for the protection of the King, who, young, inexperienced and orthodox, acted as peacemaker between the angry contestants. Wolsey, too, had ample reason to support him, for Wolsey stood on both sides. At this time Henry had no motives for staging an attack on the privileges and jurisdiction of the Church, but the affair gave him ample information for later use; from this point he knew all too well the weight of lay support he would receive in the event of a clash between Church and State.

During the disputations, Henry had declared that 'Kings of England have never had any superior but God alone', yet such phraseology had been used by his predecessors even in the fourteenth century, and he cannot thereby be credited with any revolutionary plans. Six years later he published his book exalting the primacy of the see of Rome; it also contained a moving passage on the indissolubility of Christian marriage! The prophetic character of the Hunne crisis can indeed be exaggerated. Despite the unique position and growing unpopularity of Wolsey, the period between these disputes and the meeting of the Reformation Parliament in 1529 did not seem to contemporaries one of impending cataclysm for the English Church. Its majestic institutional structure stood inviolate. Buttressed by a formidable range of institutions and laws, it supervised society concurrently with the State. Alongside Parliament, the clergy met in Convocation to debate canons and to vote clerical taxation to the King. The innumerable Church courts, archiepiscopal, episcopal, archidiaconal and peculiar, regulated not merely ecclesiastical administration and clerical conduct, but also the morals of laymen, even to the point of controlling the testamentary disposition of their personal property. Especially were these courts concerned with matrimonial causes and sexual misdemeanours, the staple fare of so many of their act books which have come down to us from the sixteenth century. And while their punishments were milder than those of the lay courts, their procedure was slow and vexatious in the extreme. The canon law they administered was based largely upon papal decrees and the canons of international Councils of the Church. National custom had also its place; our law of tithe, for example, had extensive peculiarities, while the testamentary jurisdiction of the English Church was unique in scope. Yet such details did not fundamentally alter the international character of this code, the living symbol of a great *enclave* in the sovereignty of the English State.

During the Hunne case and its sequels, those old enemies of clerical power, the common lawyers, had figured prominently, and it was into this profession that Thomas Cromwell moved some time during the years in which little is known of him. We know nothing of his legal studies and early practice, but by 1520 he must already have acquired a reputation in London, since in that year he reported to Wolsey as Papal Legate on a suit involving an appeal to Rome. Three years later he drafted a petition to Wolsey as Chancellor for the grammarian John Palsgrave. Other letters of 1520–24 show him at work as a solicitor and, on one occasion, as a trusted arbitrator in a dispute between an alderman of Calais and Lord Mountjoy. In the latter year he became a member of Gray's Inn; he was now mixing with many influential men, and trading activities were taking a less important place in his life. Which of these friends secured him a seat in the Parliament of 1523 we do not know. During this session he framed, and very possibly delivered, a long and able speech which survives in the handwriting of one of his clerks. It suggests that he had not yet entered into Wolsey's service, since his main aim is to protest against the French campaign and the large subsidies which at this moment Wolsey was demanding from the Commons. Cromwell professes himself distressed at the thought that the King may campaign in person, for if the King be lost, the country will face the horrors of civil war. Before entering a Continental war of aggression, let England first ensure her own safety, especially on the side of Scotland. The renewal of an out-of-date strategy may exhaust all the coin of the realm to the point where a leather coinage may become necessary. Let us employ Fabian tactics with the French; let us strike at them by unifying England and Scotland, a feat within our powers and one which will bring the King more glory than any of his predecessors have attained.

Cromwell's detractors have regarded this speech as the adroit attempt of a climber to rise by flattering the King. On the contrary, this is an opposition-speech, which could scarcely commend Cromwell as a willing instrument of the Crown; moreover, it is a transparently sincere criticism of the effete, backward-looking aspects of early Henrician foreign policy and closely foreshadows Cromwell's actual policy when he came to power. Here in fact is revealed an independent, businesslike, modern mind, and if, as seems unlikely, it helped to promote Cromwell, this promotion would have been by the path of honour. And awkwardly for the critics, it was in Wolsey's service, not in that of the King, that Cromwell came to spend the succeeding years.

An even more absurd misrepresentation has clung to the other document proving Cromwell's participation in this Parliament. In a private letter to his friend John Creke, Cromwell says: 'I amongst others have endured a Parliament which continued by the space of seventeen whole weeks, where we communed of war, peace, strife, contention, debate, murmur, grudge, riches, poverty, penury, truth, falsehood, justice, equity, deceit, oppression, magnanimity, activity, force, "attempraunce", treason, murder, felony, conciliation, and also how a commonwealth might be edified and also continued within our realm. Howbeit in conclusion we have done as our predecessors have been wont to do, that is to say, as well as we might, and left where we began.' The solemn scholars who have elevated this Rabelaisian catalogue into a proof of Cromwell's disbelief in parliamentary government —a notion to which his whole official career effectively gives the lie—may safely be left to the judgement of posterity. Can any member of Parliament have felt otherwise at the close of a long session? Whatever the owls of Minerva may suppose, English humour did not altogether perish between Chaucer and Shakespeare; in Cromwell it was reinforced by an admirably sardonic insight, perhaps sharpened by a touch of Italianate sophistication. And readers familiar with Tudor political treatises will at once recognize the sententious pomposity which Cromwell satirizes. He was in all respects a man of the world.

If Cromwell in fact delivered his critical speech, it did not noticeably check the development of his legal and business activities as an agent of the Cardinal. In 1524–5 petitioners for the latter's favour are seen addressing their initial pleas to the 'right worshipful Mr. Cromwell', who is now also spoken of as 'counsellor to my Lord Legate'. In becoming a member of Wolsey's household, Cromwell entered a milieu of the utmost importance to his future career. It was the nursery of the court, the training ground of future administrators and ambassadors; though inevitably it contained many clergymen, its emphasis lay on service to the State rather than to the Church. 'August and happy house', cried Erasmus, 'O truly splendid Cardinal, who has such men in his councils, and whose table is ringed by such luminaries'. As the later correspondence indicates, this household gave Cromwell a unique introduction to the men destined to prominence during the next decade. He who best knew the Cardinal's circle during the twenties was best placed to dominate English public life in the thirties. But the service proved educative in more senses than one. Wolsey's arrogance and wealth, his financial demands, his enormous combination of powers as Chancellor and Legate, his invasion of all men's jurisdictions, these and many other aspects of his career had vastly augmented the trend of the age towards anticlericalism. Wolsey made even clergymen anticlerical. Though the sequel was to show Cromwell's personal loyalty to his master, he obviously did not escape the prevailing mood. A self-made layman who had risen by the hard road, he was now in daily contact and rivalry with the most ambitious and pampered clerics of the day. Inevitably he developed a resentment towards their pretensions and their easy success; doubtless too a businessman's desire to rationalize the hoary anomalies, inefficiencies and inequities of ecclesiastical life. Just as great anticlericals like Lorenzo Valla had flourished in the heart of the papal curia, so there sat at Wolsey's table a man destined in a few years to smash the system which Wolsey had striven to revitalize through his own wonderful career.

Chapter Two

The Way to Power

WHILE Cromwell was serving Wolsey, the English Church lay under attack by forces quite distinct from those we have grouped under the label of anticlericalism. If on a certain day in 1527 Cromwell had walked a few steps from his house and entered a chamber in the Austin Friars, he could have witnessed an historic spectacle: two Essex Lollards visiting Friar Robert Barnes and coming away with a printed copy of Tyndale's forbidden New Testament in English. Going up to the friar's room, the Essex men found several people there, including a merchant reading a book. They related to Barnes how they had begun to convert the curate of their village, Steeple Bumpstead, to the Wycliffite heresy, and they went on to show him a copy of certain books of their old manuscript Lollard Bible. Barnes began to tease them concerning these antiquated exhibits and, after some adroit sales-talk, ended by selling them a copy of Tyndale's new version for 3s. 2d., 'and desired them that they would keep it close'. This scene forms one of several known and fascinating contacts between the old English and the new German heresies. Robert Barnes was a D.D. of Cambridge, who in earlier years had presided at some of the famous discussions in the 'White Horse'. About the year 1518 at this Cambridge tavern—later known as 'Little Germany'—English Lutheranism had begun a mild and academic infancy. By the time when the Essex Lollards called, the bumptious and indiscreet Barnes must already have been known to his neighbour Cromwell, since in the previous year he had been examined by Wolsey and forced to abjure heretical beliefs. In 1528 he was to escape to Antwerp and spend a long period at Luther's feet in Wittenberg. Three years later began his recorded connections with Cromwell, for it was the latter who recalled him and subsequently used him as envoy to the Lutheran princes of Germany. Their lives were henceforth closely connected to the end.

Also during the year 1527 Thomas Garret, the friend and ultimate fellow-martyr of Barnes, underwent perilous adventures in creating the first Lutheran cell at Oxford. He even had the temerity to operate in Wolsey's own new college, then being perfected by Cromwell. Before the end of the year the Bishop of Lincoln's commissary forcibly broke up this Oxford circle. Yet neither Barnes nor Garret was the great man of early English Lutheranism. William Tyndale, whose translation of the New Testament they were both engaged in selling, had left the country for Wittenberg as early as 1524 and, financed in all likelihood by a group of London cloth-merchants, was shipping his first edition into England two years later. It was the work of a harsh and angular Protestant, who used loaded terminology and linked the sacred text with a series of violently controversial prologues and marginal notes. It also happened to be a work of genius, the ancestor and basis of all the early versions in English. So translated, the New Testament needed no partisan embellishments to become an explosive force. Everywhere in England people seem to have been curious about it, and at whatever point one examines the social history of the early Reformation in England, the Tyndale version makes its presence felt. For many a reader it meant a fresh awakening, a new, personal and direct approach to truths long staled by too circuitous a presentation. There can be little doubt that it also meant something to Cromwell, for, as we shall later observe, he was already in 1527 discussing the scriptures with another Augustinian friar, who had already attained some notoriety for defending Barnes. This was Miles Coverdale, a name destined to take second place only to that of Tyndale in the annals of the English Bible.

Having turned aside to glance at Cromwell's neighbour Barnes, we must not allow the Essex Lollards to smuggle out their copy of Tyndale and vanish without further notice into the busy streets of London. Recent research into diocesan archives indicates with increasing clarity what a more careful study of Foxe would earlier have revealed: that Lollardy, so far from being, as Gairdner supposed, a spent force on the eve of the Reformation, survived in some strength to prepare the ground for Protestantism. The beliefs deriving from Wyclif were more radically Protestant than those of Luther himself; they seem the forerunners if not the parents of English Nonconformity. They exalted the Bible as the sole criterion of faith; they attacked the Pope, the episcopal hierarchy, the worship of saints, the doctrine of purgatory and, above all, belief in transubstantiation. If historians still venture to notice conscious motivations in history, they must surely agree that the Reformation centred around the sacrament of the altar, around the validity of belief in the corporal presence of Christ's body in the bread and wine of the eucharist. Constituted an article of faith at the Lateran Council of 1215, transubstantiation had been further elaborated in consonance with the fashionable Aristotelianism of that day, whereby the 'accidents' or outward appearance of the elements remained unchanged, while their 'substance' was transformed. Late Lollardy, going farther than either Wyclif or Luther, denied the real presence in its entirety. Here was the heresy of heresies, for which men continued to be consigned to the flames until the end of the reign of Henry VIII, then once again under Mary Tudor.

Lollardy had undergone several regional persecutions in the early decades of the century. In the diocese of London, mainly in Essex, Bishop Fitzjames prosecuted about 50 Lollards in 1510 and about as many in 1518. Between 1527 and 1532 his successors Tunstall and Stokesley caused well over 200 heretics, mainly Lollards, to abjure. In the Chilterns, especially around Amersham, sizeable attacks were made by the Bishops of Lincoln in 1506–7 and in 1521. Another centre lay in south-west Kent, where Archbishop Warham became very active in 1511; the Chiltern and Kentish groups were connected by a scattering of Lollards up the Thames valley to Newbury, where six or seven score abjurations took place in the early years of the century. During each of these intermittent drives a few Lollards suffered burning, but in general the movement survived by secretiveness and flexibility rather than by heroism. Its importance lay, not merely in these organized communities, but in its ability to permeate even the remoter parts of England wth diffused beliefs of anti-hierarchical and anti-sacramental character. In the incomplete records of the York diocesan courts, the present writer recently found and examined 33 heresy-cases between 1528 and 1543, besides another 45 in the reign of Mary. At both periods the great majority—those on the proletarian level—remained purely Lollard in character, similar, in fact, to scores of pre-

Lutheran cases. It would seem that by the early thirties the influence of Lutheranism in the provinces was still virtually limited to a minority of educated and half-educated persons, and that in the broad psychological preparation of the English people we must now accord a far from minor role to the operations of the old English heresy. This fact in no way implies that people like Cromwell ever entertained warm sympathies with Lollard radicalism. So far as respectable people were concerned, Lollards remained rank outsiders, and before long every moderate Reformer found himself compelled to ward off any suspicion of sympathy with sacramentarian extremism, whether it derived from Lollardy or from Anabaptism, which latter began during the thirties to percolate from the Netherlands into London and the southeastern counties.

While in the service of the Cardinal, Cromwell occasionally rubbed shoulders with men like Coverdale, yet he can have had little time for doctrinal study or speculation, since he soon became one of the busiest administrators in England. From 1525 until the cataclysm of 1529, Wolsey chiefly employed Cromwell on the project nearest his heart: the suppression of some twenty-nine minor monasteries in order to erect two great colleges at Oxford and Ipswich. In surveying the monastic properties, making inventories of goods, transferring lands, meeting the claims of tenants, drawing up foundation-deeds, building and furnishing the new colleges, Cromwell executed with brilliance a task of enormous legal ramifications and administrative complexity. No lease was too petty for close inspection; no consignment of furniture too trivial for personal supervision. That Wolsey's transfer was an act of genuine enlightenment will be denied by few observers. It involved no doctrinal principles and it received active support from Stephen Gardiner and other ecclesiastics noted in later years for their conservative opinions. It was by no means the first transaction of its kind, for many years earlier Bishops Alcock and Fisher had suppressed religious houses in order to found Cambridge colleges. It subtracted extremely little from the wealth of the religious orders: while it may have contributed to Wolsey's unpopularity, he had already become so widely unpopular in both clerical and lay circles that its political importance deserves little emphasis.

Along with the lesser agents of the Cardinal, Cromwell accepted from interested parties numerous gifts, which would be regarded as gross bribes in the case of a modern administrator, but which then, and for long afterwards, formed the normal perquisites of unpaid or underpaid officials. These early gifts were matters of common knowledge, and Wolsey himself must certainly have permitted them; with reason, since as a layman Cromwell could not be rewarded by the shower of lucrative benefices which fell upon less important officials in Holy Orders. Even when he came to enjoy offices under the Crown, Cromwell disdained no present, large or small; he maintained no secrecy and little subtlety in these matters; he continued to behave as the enterprising businessman, intent to ensure that the acceptance of expensive public office did not restrain the mounting profits which had rewarded his earlier career. One who has followed modern research through the mercenary intrigues of the Tudor political scene will end, not by condemning Cromwell as corrupt, but rather by placing amongst the saintly eccentrics of their age those few sensitive consciences he may encounter. It is the misfortune of many Tudor statesmen to be judged by the exceptional criterion of Sir Thomas More. From the viewpoint of his employers, Cromwell gave far more than current value in return for his extensive pickings. At no stage of this or any later negotiation did he spare himself long hours, hard thinking, wearisome journeys, application to dull detail and a life of complete dedication to the task in hand. His was the administrative genius built on a capacity for taking infinite pains, and on this scale such genius proved a great rarity amongst Tudor Englishmen.

From this time onwards, Cromwell succeeded in making himself the chief lay expert upon the English monasteries, and an extensive book on their last stages could be compiled solely from his correspondence. The scene which presented itself to him in the years following 1525 contained some strange anomalies and problems. Its extant records are remarkably voluminous, while the size and romantic appeal of monastic ruins have also helped to inflate the theme to such proportions that many observers have been unable to view Thomas Cromwell in any other context. Yet the splendours of Fountains and Rievaulx form dangerous guides to the realities destroyed by Cromwell, for the architecture was out of all proportion to the religious lives which it housed. After their early triumphs, the English had not shown themselves conspicuously gifted in this vocation, and by the reign of Henry VIII the number of English religious had become pitifully small, both absolutely and by comparison with those on the Continent. Dr. Gasquet computes at the dissolution 4,721 monks and regular canons, 1,800 friars and only 1,560 nuns. The 357 lesser monasteries attacked in 1536 averaged scarcely four religious persons each, a figure which explains at least one important aspect of the disciplinary and educational problem. At the opposite extreme, the bigger establishments tended to be hampered by debt and overheads, especially by the upkeep of their grandiose buildings. Some maintained swollen domestic staffs. Butley Priory in Suffolk had only twelve canons, but it also kept two chaplains, eleven personal servants, a barber, a schoolmaster, seven schoolchildren, three cooks, a slaughterman, a sacristan, a cooper, three bakers and brewers, two horsekeepers, two maltsters, a porter, a gardener, six laundresses and two bedemen; all these quite part from an understeward, a surveyor and 36 workers on the Butley estate.

The disciplinary state of the religious houses holds few mysteries, since considerable reliance may be placed upon innumerable visitation reports compiled by the bishops. Even so, these documents demand cautious treatment; they give little prominence to the many virtuous denizens who were dutifully maintaining their vows; they concentrate on faults; they are confidential reports based on the obligation of each member to divulge all misdemeanours in private interview with the bishop. No other social group has had to confront so fierce a scrutiny. Moreover, as we peruse the records of a house across thirty years, we gain a foreshortened view of its defects; during such a period a few offences and feuds, even serious ones, do not make it a sink of iniquity. Even, however, when due allowance has been made for all these factors, the episcopal visitations reveal many inadequacies which would not for a moment be tolerated in any modern religious order. We should do wrong to concentrate upon the sensational establishments like Dorchester, with its ceaseless quarrels, its openness to the public and its alleged sexual offences; or like Littlemore, where the prioress lived with a former chaplain, endowed her illegitimate daughter with the convent goods and put her nuns in the stocks; or like Walsingham, where the prior was charged with an amazing range of offences, had his faction amongst the deep-drinking canons, and committed management to the lay seneschal's wife, a crony of the heartier canons and reputedly the prior's mistress. In the average place,

27

the occasional misfit may indeed crop up over the years: the canon who wanders off in criminal company, the nun who has a baby. Considering the folly with which most orders accepted immature professions and then attempted at all costs to retain the maladjusted, the wonder is that such cases did not prove far more numerous.

The really characteristic faults of monks and nuns were more venial in character: irregular attendance at the divine offices, addiction to private property and lay dress, uncharity towards their fellows, and disharmony between the heads of houses and their rank-and-file. Much trouble arose from excessive familiarity with the surrounding lay world. For this fault the hypocritical laity deserved a large share of the blame, since their exploitation of monastic amenities, offices and properties had reached intolerable proportions. During the years 1534–6 the correspondence of Thomas Cromwell contains, amongst a mountain of similar material, many letters from the factions in and around Whitby Abbey. At this picturesque but disorderly institution, Abbot Hexham took his cut in the proceeds of piracy, while his servants waged ruffianly battles with the fishermen in the town below. More serious complications arose from the factions of the local gentry, who tried to operate both through Cromwell and by means of local violence. The young puritan magnate Sir Francis Bigod backed the bailiff James Conyers, while the rival family of Eure supported his enemy and kinsman Gregory Conyers. The first of these factions was leagued with a reforming group of monks, who almost succeeded in unseating Hexham; yet at the same time Bigod, desperately in need of ready cash despite his large estates, borrowed money, not only from Cromwell and the London financiers, but also from his adversary Hexham. This story of chicanery and violence, with the scores finally paid off in the Pilgrimage of Grace, might be warmly commended to any historical novelist.

Some of the less dramatic stories are equally illuminating. The chronicle of Butley Priory provides typical examples of lay interference with a well-conducted house. Here the King's gay sister Mary, dowager-Queen of France and Duchess of Suffolk, spent three summer vacations with her train of ladies and gentlemen. Here she hunted the fox in Staverton Park, supped with the flattered canons in their little private gardens, and once, driven indoors by a storm, hastened to finish her supper in the monastic church. On another occasion her husband Suffolk planted the members of his private chapel upon the house, which proceeded to keep them for nine months. And Butley was not the only East Anglian priory used as a cheap hotel by this handsome and popular couple.

As with the secular clergy, the intellectual achievements of the last generation of medieval monks permit of little easy generalization. Centuries ago, the monasteries had ceased to afford cultural leadership; the best had become parasitic upon the universities, while the worst had sunk rather boorishly into their bucolic settings. The two liveliest traditions in early Tudor intellectual life were the humanism of Italy and the Quietist piety of the Lower Rhineland, which latter had its classic in the *Imitatio Christi* and its English parallels in Richard Rolle and his literary successors. In writings and library catalogues emanating from the English monasteries, these two developments are rather sparsely represented, perhaps the brightest exceptions being the maintenance of the humanist tradition at Christ Church, Canterbury, and of the mystical tradition in the small Carthusian Order. Academic education continued to attract monks at least as powerfully as in any earlier period: the houses of studies kept by various orders at the two universities continued well-filled, and many hundreds of monks figure on the university registers during the last thirty years. Though there was little intellectual scope for educated monks when they returned to their houses, the latter nevertheless contained some men of literary talent like Andrew Boorde and Alexander Barclay, as well as a few deservedly popular devotional writers like William Bond and Richard Whitford.

In the field of popular education, religious houses played no more than a minor role. Monastic cathedrals like Norwich and Worcester had small schools; St. Mary's, York, used some of its ample revenues to keep a boarding-house for fifty boys at the neighbouring cathedral school, while certain smaller houses kept schoolmasters for their young monks and for a few children of their officers and neighbours. Despite these and other exceptions, English education suffered extremely little by the dissolution. On the other hand, monastic hospitality was widely if indiscriminately extended to callers ranging from dukes to sturdy beggars: particular houses like Sawley Abbey in the wild Pennine country conferred valuable services on travellers. It is hard to estimate the precise impact of monastic largesse upon social life. Its critics blamed it for the prevalence of vagabondage, but it was probably not large enough to exert major economic influences. The *Valor Ecclesiasticus*, that great survey of ecclesiastical income organized in 1535 by Thomas Cromwell, records monastic charities amounting only to $2\frac{1}{2}$ per cent. of gross income, but this survey is concerned solely with disbursements and doles which the monks were obliged to make by the provisions of pious benefactors. For all we know, the monks may have given as much again out of pure goodwill, but this would seem a large assumption in view of the debts and financial struggles which beset most houses during the last decades.

Similar considerations apply also to monastic landlordism. All the available evidence suggests that the attitude of ecclesiastical lords to tenants, workmen and neighbours closely resembled that of their lay neighbours. The reports of Wolsey's enclosure commissioners show numerous monasteries charged with enclosure and eviction of tenants. Stray allusions continually support this evidence. The chronicler of Butley Priory, for example, records a riot in 1526 by the men of Orford against enclosures made by the Priory on what they claimed as common land, while in 1517 the Abbot of Peterborough became involved in prolonged legal struggles against the townsmen on account of enclosures forcibly made by him upon the Fens. Sir Thomas More included 'certain abbots, holy men no doubt' amongst the people responsible for harsh enclosures. No agrarian Elysium therefore existed on monastic estates, nor did contemporaries make this claim on their behalf. Some slight idealization inevitably occurs in later literature, but it lacks first-hand character and is unimpressive in scope and intensity. In general, monasteries had always been tenacious, sometimes unscrupulous, in asserting all their legal rights, and the immense number of proceedings brought against them in Chancery from the fourteenth century to the dissolution proves this fact to the hilt.

In fairness, it should be recalled that their financial obligations were heavy and that they often needed to protect themselves against neighbours even more unscrupulous and acquisitive. Again, the fact that laymen as stewards and bailiffs had an influential voice in their policy must help to account for its close assimilation to the general pattern. The greatest men in the realm did not disdain these offices. The Earl of Shrewsbury held at least eleven monastic stewardships, the Earl of Derby seven, the Earls of Rutland and Wiltshire six each. By the time of the dissolution Thomas Cromwell's four or five did much less than justice to his now unique position in the monastic world. By then he was appointing the heads of houses; he corresponded with a vast number of them on intimate terms, while accepting their annuities and gifts right and left. His memory was exact and tenacious, his knowledge of monasticism extensive and peculiar. But Cromwell had only just concluded his apprenticeship in this field of administration when Wolsey, having failed to provide the King with his divorce, fell from power.

The momentous change of October 1529 threw the Cardinal's chief administrative agent into profound anxiety. In terms of material possessions he had become a substantial man with much to lose. The text of the will compiled by him in the previous July gives no complete picture of his lands and properties, but he makes over thirty cash bequests amounting to about £1,600, then a large sum and matched only in the wills of the richer London merchants. Had Cromwell died at this moment, he would have gone down, if not to national history, at least to the social antiquities of London as a mundane but considerate character, notable for his family piety and highly practical beneficence. Besides remembering a host of relatives, friends and servants, he leaves £20 to the making of highways, £40 for sixty doweries to poor maidens, £20 to poor house holders to pray for his soul, £10 to poor parishioners, £10 to prisoners in Newgate, Ludgate, the King's Bench and Marshalsea prisons, and £5 to the five orders of friars to pray for him. This last relatively meagre bequest indicates, however, no scepticism concerning masses for the dead, since he also orders his executors to hire an honest *and continent* priest to sing for his soul for seven years at a cost of £46 13s. 4d. Within a few weeks of drafting these provisions, Cromwell must have begun to doubt whether in fact he would manage to retain this fortune; whether at any rate his ambitions for further advancement were not doomed. According to Pole, a rumour circulated in London at this time that Cromwell had been sent to the Tower for execution. His friend and business-associate Stephen Vaughan showed himself deeply perturbed, and Cromwell himself certainly feared to be sucked down with the great ecclesiastical galleon to which he had entrusted his fortunes. Then came the moment of decision which brought him safely out of the vortex. The story of this critical moment cannot be told otherwise than in the words of George Cavendish, who had that power of observation sometimes vouchsafed to good and simple spirits, and whose biography of Wolsey forms so signal a triumph of character over intellect.

On All Hallows day 1529, when Wolsey had been relegated to retirement at Esher, Cavendish chanced to see Cromwell there in the great chamber, 'leaning in the great window with a Primer in his hand, saying our Lady matins: which had been a strange sight in him afore. . . . He prayed no more earnestly than he distilled tears as fast from his eyes. Whom I saluted and bade good-morrow. And with that I perceived his moist cheeks, the which he wiped with his napkin. To whom I said, " Why, Mr. Cromwell, what meaneth this dole? Is my lord in any danger that you do lament for him, or is it for any other loss, that you have sustained by misfortune?" "Nay," quoth he, "it is for my unhappy adventure. For I am like to lose all that I have laboured for, all the days of my life, for doing of my master true and diligent service." "Why sir," quoth I, "I trust that you be too wise to do anything by my lord's commandment otherwise than you might do, whereof you ought to be in doubt or danger for loss of your goods." "Well, well," quoth he, "I cannot tell; but this I see before mine eyes, that everything is as it is taken; and this I know well, that I am disdained withal for my master's sake; and yet I am sure there is no cause, why they should do so. An evil name once gotten will not lightly be put away. I never had promotion by my lord to the increase of my living. But this much I will say to you, that I will this afternoon, when my lord has dined, ride to London, and to the court, when I will either make or mar, ere ever I come again. I will put myself in prease, to see what they will be able to lay to my charge." "Mary," quoth I, "then in so doing you shall do wisely, beseeching God to send you good luck, as I would myself." '

The immediate sequel proved equally revealing of Cromwell's character and outlook. Though in crisis he had turned to conventional devotions, he had a strong partiality for the laymen of the household and a distaste for the priests, who had become the real beneficiaries of their master's worldly success. When the Cardinal had said mass, he dined with Cromwell and his chaplains, and during dinner the former told Wolsey that he ought to assemble his faithful gentlemen and yeomen, and express to them his thanks and commendation, a gesture which would encourage them to sustain the common misfortune. 'Alas, Thomas,' replied Wolsey, 'ye know I have nothing to give them, and words without deeds be not often well taken.' But Cromwell continued with his customary bluntness that Wolsey had made his chaplains rich with benefices, some being now able to spend a thousand marks a year, and none less than three hundred. While these clergymen had got all the profit, the laymen had nothing, 'and yet hath your poor servants taken much more pains for you in one day than all your idle chaplains hath done in a year'. The Cardinal agreed, and so Cromwell ordered Cavendish to assemble the gentlemen along one side of the great chamber, the yeomen along the other. As they all stood there weeping—in the way strong men did not scruple to do in Tudor times—Wolsey conquered his own emotions and made them a long speech of thanks. This done, Cromwell, still intent to champion their interests and to shame the chaplains, suggested that the latter should subscribe money to send off the laymen on a month's holiday, by which time the King's decision and the fate of the household would be known. Surely, the charity of the chaplains was not so void of grace that they would see the Cardinal lack when they might help him! 'And for my part, although I have not received of your Grace's gift one penny towards the increase of my yearly living, yet will I depart [share] with you this towards the dispatch of your servants.' With these words, Cromwell gave Wolsey five pounds in gold. 'And now let us see', he continued, 'what your chaplains will do. I think they will depart with you much more than I have done, who be more able to give you a pound than I one penny.' Turning to the chaplains (whose thoughts cannot by this time have been very charitable) he added sardonically, 'Go to, masters!' They had no alternative but to meet the challenge, some giving ten pounds and some less, but in the end raising enough to send off the servants with a quarter's wages. This done, the Cardinal returned to his chamber, lamenting the departure of his servants, 'making his moan unto Master Cromwell, who comforted him the best he could, and desired my lord to give him leave to go to London, where he he would either make or mar ere he came again, which was always his common saying'. After a long and secret conversation with Wolsey, Cromwell then took horse for London with his clerk Ralph Sadler, bidding Cavendish farewell with the words, 'Ye shall hear shortly of me, and if I speed well, I will not fail to be here again within these two days'.

The adventurer was as good as his word. A few days later he returned 'with a pleasant countenance' and told Cavendish that he had dared 'to put his feet where he would be better regarded, ere ever the Parliament was finished'. He had in fact obtained the approval of the King and the Duke of Norfolk to become a burgess, and through the good offices of Sir William Paulet, a former fellow-servant of Wolsey, he sat in the first session of the Reformation Parliament as member for Taunton. Here, as Cavendish again shows, he defended the fallen Wolsey and ensured that the Bill of Attainder brought against him would be dropped. He also took a hand in organizing the resentment of his fellow-members against the power and privileges of the Church. It has been demonstrated by Dr. Elton that the first drafts of the document known as the Supplication against the Ordinaries not only contain Cromwell's corrections, but date from the year 1529, three years before this powerful attack upon ecclesiastical jurisdiction and the legislative powers of Convocation was actually delivered. It was hence a genuine House of Commons document, and its early history shows that Cromwell's skill as a draftsman had already obtained recognition by the powerful anticlerical group in the House.

In short, within a few weeks he had begun to win good opinions in a new field and to build up a second career upon the ruins of the first. Until shortly before Wolsey's death, Cromwell, even while he gave careful thought to his own ambitions, continued to work hard on the affairs of his former master. If he was gradually disengaging himself during the year 1530, staying longer at court and dancing attendance less and less upon the querulous old prelate, his conduct throughout these exchanges was marked by far more decency and consideration than that of Wolsey's other former supporters, including Stephen Gardiner himself. Some of his letters at this time show a reverence and an affection for Wolsey as obviously heartfelt as anything in Tudor correspondence. On this score Merriman and other modern biographers excel themselves in prejudice. When Cromwell alone speaks up in Parliament for the Cardinal and gains for him a temporary pardon, this can only have been to gain a reputation for faithfulness; if he fails to prevent the seizure of Wolsey's colleges, then he is no true servant. When Cromwell writes Wolsey

34

a long, news-laden and, as it seems to me, polite letter of consolation, this becomes in Merriman's eyes 'empty' and 'almost contemptuous'. By implication at least, Cromwell even incurs blame for not defying the King and Norfolk at the time of the final attack upon the doomed Cardinal. The reader soon begins to realize that nothing short of a Cromwell who vainly offered up his whole career on Wolsey's funeral pyre would have sufficed to satisfy these faithful followers of the black legend.

To prosper in Tudor times, a man needed to get lordship as much as in the previous chaotic century of the Pastons, and the royal service now presented itself to Cromwell as obviously the most desirable. Many of Wolsey's servants had, on the express advice of their master, long preceded him in making the transfer, which usually involved a formal, quasi-feudal oath. It has been shown that Cromwell must have taken this between 17 December 1529, and April 1530, although until Wolsey's death, in the following November, Cromwell's letters refer almost solely to his own and the Cardinal's affairs. At some date before 10 January, 1531, he was sworn of the King's Council; during this and the subsequent year, leading officials and noblemen sought his help and favours in respectful terms. As yet, however, he was no policy-maker, but a mere executive agent for the King's legal and financial affairs; he took grants of land to the King's use, supervised the drafting and sealing of indentures concerning Crown lands, received sums for building the King's tomb, consulted with the law officers on various aspects of royal business, superintended the collection of clerical subsidies and the revenues of vacant sees. Even now, he was not above a little modest business enterprise of his own. As late as February 1532 Stephen Vaughan was selling some spermaceti for him in Antwerp and complaining that it put him to more pain than anything he ever had to sell, since it was rapidly putrifying and 'subtilly packed, being nothing so good within as without'.

We know little of the personal relationships between the King and Cromwell during the years 1531–2, but the outcome shows that he made good use of his frequent access to the presence, and that Henry speedily came to see in him the high-powered executive able to replace the Duke of Norfolk and the other fumbling amateurs who had overthrown Wolsey, yet lacked the professional experience and the application to assume his functions. When there developed in Parliament a new crisis in papal and ecclesiastical affairs, the hand of Cromwell can first be felt in the sphere of high policy. He had at last arrived, and for eight years both Church and State in England received a guidance infinitely more forceful and far-seeing than at any time between the death of Henry VII and the advent of Cecil.

The personality which had emerged at the end of this long and arduous road seems to me somewhat complex. It corresponds all too little with the rash phrases used by Cromwell's simplifying critics. His portraits in the Bodleian, in the Frick and in the National Portrait Gallery do not in themselves carry us far. The second and third of these show someone not unlike the conventional Cromwell: the administrator, thin-lipped, narrow-eyed, astute, responsible, never yielding a point without calculation. Contemporaries add to these characteristics a short heavy build and an uncouth gait; at times the impression of a patient and somewhat wooden character. These were superficial notions. Chapuys, by no means concerned to flatter, remarks that his countenance was extremely mobile, and that when he became engaged in a conversation of interest, his face would suddenly light up, the dull expression yielding to a subtle, cunning and intelligent aspect. At such moments, his conversation became extraordinarily witty and entertaining; he then had a habit of giving a roguish, oblique glance whenever he made a smart remark. The only portrait suggesting this animated Cromwell is that in the Bodleian; here he seems for the moment the serious but sardonic listener, who in a second or two will flash out a piece of repartee.

By this time his career had taught him self-control in its various forms. Each rung of the ladder had been slippery, and as every Tudor courtier and moralist knew, the least reliable rung was the one at the top. In the courts of princes the smooth surfaces of formal address masked rampant jealousy and treachery; for all the bows and titles, men fought like animals for pre-eminence, privilege and wealth. Even those born near the summit had to be cunning, cautious, adaptable. How much more so the rare man who had risen from the bottom and had been entrusted with the least popular tasks of government! Life became infinitely calculating; he must learn when to be humble, when to be ha·d, when to be sociable, when to take advantage of an opponent's weakness. If such a man had been educated in Italy, he might have developed the explicitly low view of human nature in the manner of Machiavelli or of Guicciardini, and seldom can he have found occasion to take a view more elevated. Cromwell, as the letters of his correspondents show even more clearly than his own, was the precise opposite of the flint-faced automaton of legend. On the contrary, he was infinitely adaptable to human nature, all things to all men. One would say he possessed a genius for friendship, if one did not suspect that too many of his friendships were dedicated to the purpose of his career, his ministry and his mission.

He was a good mixer and even in the days of his power his correspondents do not address him as an ogre, but as a highly approachable magnate, one who preferred to be tackled frankly and who, if he could so act without injuring himself, would readily do them good turns. Surrounded by enterprising suppliants, he can scarcely be blamed for getting services in return for many of these favours, since here was the bond by which Tudor government subsisted. No English minister has ever bound so many men of all sorts and conditions to himself; a great institutional organizer, he also contrived to gain intimate personal relationships with a surprisingly large section of the ruling and middle classes. Satirical, witty, sometimes openly cynical, he must also have known when to avoid the harsh jest, for his friends of longer standing were by no means backward in confiding to him their most intimate problems and aspirations. That early puritan Sir Francis Bigod confessed to him in emotional terms that he felt his mission in life was to preach sermons, and he besought Cromwell to license him to be a married priest, or else something equally sensational: a lay preacher. In a small group of old friends like Stephen Vaughan, Cromwell certainly inspired sentiments which look uncommonly like affection. Conversely, the highly organized life of a first minister with a whole gamut of lesser offices ended by gravely limiting the chance of disinterested friendships. Too much of this type of dedication seems good for nobody: we have all met the eminent public administrator in middle age, gaining in suave precision as he loses the capacity for personal affection, ever in danger of seeing his associates as pawns in the institutional game. Even before he reached this stage, Cromwell sometimes showed the aggressive touch of the sharp businessman. In his *Survey of London* Stow relates how Cromwell built his house in Throgmorton Street near the Austin Friars and, intent to enlarge his garden, took down the pales of the neighbouring gardens, measured twenty-two feet into what they claimed as their land, erected a brick wall along this new line and removed on rollers a shed belonging to Stow's father. Cromwell had no doubt acquired some legal title to this land, but it is evident that he chose to assert it in an arbitrary manner. It is fair to add here that Stow also recalls having seen when a boy more than two hundred poor fed twice a day at Cromwell's gate.

He was certainly loyal and generous towards people who had helped him in his struggling days. Whatever the hostility of public opinion in the remoter provinces, Cromwell enjoyed a certain popularity in London. On his fall in 1540 his arrest was kept secret and sudden, since the government feared trouble in the city. His scaffold was carefully guarded; a war of broadside ballads arose over his death and had to be suppressed by the Council. Foxe tells a whole series of anecdotes to illustrate his liberality and the good turns done by him to people of whom Foxe approved. His enemies alleged that he was unpopular amongst the lords and gentry because he was a 'great taker and briber' like Wolsey, but they admitted that 'he spent it honourably and freely like a gentleman (though he were none) and helped many honest men and preferred his servants well'.

The term Philistine has been levelled too freely against Cromwell, perhaps through mistaken impressions deriving from his cult of efficiency. It is not justified by his habits and cultural attainments. He appears indeed as a man of taste who appreciated the amenities and elegances of his age, while shunning the ostentation which had turned men against Wolsey. He was interested in the substance and purposes of power rather than in its trappings, and his mode of life represented a sensible compromise between his modest origins and his high office. Even when prime minister and among the richest men in England, he continued to live in relatively small houses. That near the Austin Friars, his favourite residence, was sumptuously furnished, and the Venetian Ambassador, who often dined there, praised everything he saw. This house, which he had bought from his friend Anthony Vivaldi, was no palace, but had a gate tower, a large dining-hall and ample kitchens. Cromwell entertained well and went to great trouble about food, having a wet and dry larder built in each of his houses. Coverdale is full of the pleasures of staying with him; even his arch-enemy Chapuys often sat at his table and remarks that on such occasions the most careful politicians were put off their guard by Cromwell's pleasing presence and address, which led them to reveal things they should have kept private.

He seems to have had that passionate love of quality in physical objects which marks many a self-made man who has had to earn them by hard work. He corresponded at length with Stephen Vaughan about an iron chest of elaborate workmanship, which was so expensive that Vaughan hesitated to purchase it for him. He also wanted to buy in Flanders for forty crowns a carved dining-table 'of such size as there are few in England'. A mutilated list of his furniture shows that, at a time when they were not widely collected in England, he had at least twelve pictures. He also purchased a globe with explanatory notes, and the only two copies of the *Cronica Cronicarum* which could be found in Antwerp. As will appear, the claim that he made Machiavelli his Bible cannot be substantiated, yet there can be no doubt that his stay in Italy had given him a love of Italian literature. In April 1530 Edmund Bonner writes to remind Cromwell of a promise to lend him the *Triumphs* of Petrarch and the *Book of the Courtier*, and 'to make him a good Italian'. Stray references suggest that he had read quite widely when time permitted. Amongst his official papers are a poem, 'Amongst all flowers the rose doth excell', a dialogue between Pasquillus and Marforius, and various Italian verses. Both before and during his prominence in public life he had innumerable friendships with literary men such as Miles Coverdale, translator of the Bible, the versatile Lord Morley, who dedicated a work to him, Thomas Elyot, famous author of *The Governor*, the brilliant humanists Richard Morison and Thomas Starkey, and John Palsgrave, who wrote one of our best early French grammars and dictionaries. His personal interest in Biblical translation and political thought will become increasingly apparent. In the days of his power he was an enthusiastic patron of scholars and writers, extremely conscious of their social importance in the swiftly-expanding world of ideas. Ample evidence indicates that such interest was far from being solely limited to the creation of political propaganda. Though his appointment in 1535 as High Steward of the University of Cambridge chiefly reflected his political influence, his relations with that University were not purely formal, since he had been maintaining scholars there as early as October 1530.

His recreations were otherwise typical of contemporary magnates. He spent large sums on singing birds, kept a small orchestra of musicians among his servants and a fool to amuse his guests, played bowls, cards and dice, sometimes losing at court very large sums. He kept nearly a hundred horses in his stables, but habitually rode a mule to and fro between his house and the court. He shot with the long bow and hunted, but his favourite sport was hawking, and he was best pleased by gifts of hawks, spaniels or greyhounds. The Spanish Ambassador went out hawking with him to get private conversation, and reports him as drawing a metaphor from the sport: 'The Emperor and his agents like hawks rise high to come down fast on their prey.'

In considering the suitability of the term Philistine, another consideration may at ths point be deduced. Those who have read the unsavoury reports made by some of his agents concerning the immoralities of monks might leap to the conclusion that Cromwell relished indecent stories. This seems a totally false inference. An English student at Padua once set him a copy of some indecent Italian verses, which he had seen stuck on a church door, but Cromwell waxed furious and the student came very near losing his exhibition. Altogether, a distinctly human being emerges from the personal details, and we shall see that a study of Cromwell's official career, even that side of it relating to his enemies, by no means convicts him of inhumanity. On the other hand, his emotional life remains obscure; its extent and depth might well be questioned, and only a bold partisan would seek to glorify his qualities in this important sphere of human character. His successive environments were all hostile towards delicacy and sensibility; in addition, he became too much the servant of an idea.

Chapter Three

The Opening Moves

SINCE 1527 the royal policy had revolved ever more narrowly around the King's plans to obtain a divorce, marry Anne Boleyn, and obtain a sorely-needed male heir to the throne. His case had from the first been clouded—and has remained so ever since—by his adulterous self-will, by his prior liaison with Anne's own sister, by his rather indecent capacity for moralistic self-deception, by his cruel animosity against a faithful, virtuous and stubborn queen. Judging him solely within the context of private ethics, little can be said in his favour, though he entertained an apparently genuine conviction that Katherine's persistent miscarriages and the deaths in infancy of all his children, save Mary, had been caused by the divine curse pronounced against marriage with a deceased brother's wife. His case in canon law was fairly strong, strong enough at least to convince many learned canonists and more than strong enough to give a veneer of decency to a political divorce based upon national necessity. The dispensation by which Pope Julius II had originally permitted the marriage of Henry and Katherine was declared by the English lawyers to be invalid on five grounds, notably since the King had been only twelve years old at the time, had not sought the dispensation, and had protested against the marriage on reaching the age of fourteen. The dispute afterwards centred upon the query as to whether Katherine and her first husband Arthur had actually cohabited: if so, it was generally held that the papal dispensation would thereby have been invalidated. Katherine herself consistently maintained that cohabitation with Arthur had never taken place, though evidence of sorts to the contrary was also produced. Judged on grounds neither of family-ethics nor of canon law, but on those of *raison d'état*, there remained every argument in favour of the King's divorce and remarriage. And in cases with no stronger legal backing than

Henry's, earlier popes had realized that kings are not as other men, and had given them the benefit of the doubt; many men could remember how Louis XII of France had been divorced by the Pope to allow of his politic marriage with the heiress of Brittany.

Pope Clement VII was an irresolute politician, anxious not to offend Henry and most amenable to worldly pressures, yet Rome had just undergone siege and sack, complete with every imaginable brutality, by the troops of Emperor Charles, King of Spain and nephew of Katherine of Aragon. When in the autumn of 1527 the French momentarily recovered power in Italy, Clement relaxed and began to grant Henry some important concessions; they included a dispensation abolishing impediments to the proposed Boleyn marriage, should the union with Katherine turn out to be invalid. In February 1528 Stephen Gardiner the King's secretary and Edward Fox his almoner, both of them formidable canonists, were sent out to augment the attack upon the unfortunate pontiff; they menaced him with the prospects of a General Council and an English schism; for the moment their threats received increasing support from the continued victories of the French. That April Clement granted a bull empowering Cardinals Wolsey and Campeggio jointly and severally to hear the case, declare, if need arose, the nullity of the marriage, license the parties to remarry and legitimize Henry's children. Since Wolsey was the King's man and Campeggio Bishop of Salisbury and Cardinal Protector of England, the prospects seemed fair indeed for the royal cause. Yet from this point everything went amiss. By the end of the year the Spanish armies once again stood in control of Italy, and Clement, relapsing into the grip of Charles, could do no more than play for time. The proceedings before Wolsey and Campeggio dawdled until July 1529, when the consolidation of Imperial control over Rome compelled the Pope to revoke their commission and summon the parties to appear in Rome. The backers of Katherine were triumphant, while to describe the outraged feelings of Henry, the term virtuous indignation would seem quite inadequate. He valued his services to Christendom very highly, and had long felt conscious that neither Providence nor the Roman curia were granting those rewards which merits so substantial might justly claim.

If the resplendent champion of the Papacy were thus fooled by a bogus trial and then called before a foreign tribunal, there could be little justice in the universe, let alone in Rome. At all events, the time had come to appeal elswhere. The resultant fall of Wolsey (who seemed useless to Henry unless he could switch on the fountain of papal jurisdiction) nevertheless accomplished strangely little: he was not succeeded by a mind with a master-plan. Government lapsed into the hands of Norfolk, Suffolk and Anne Boleyn's father Wiltshire—respectively, a soldier with a certain cunning, a handsome façade and a grasping nonentity, none of them showing the slightest claim to original and decisive statesmanship. When Cromwell became chief minister in 1532, the 'great matter' lay substantially where it had lain at Wolsey's fall. The only new step of any interest had been taken on a sug-gestion made in the autumn of 1529 by Thomas Cranmer, then still a Cambridge don, that the universities of Europe should be consulted on the divorce. This done, loyalty, pressure and bribery produced the predictable series of results. Oxford and Cambridge declared for the King, while Francis I, ever intent to strike a blow at Spain and the Habsburgs, induced the French universi-ties to do likewise. Even Bologna, nominally in papal territory, and Padua followed suit, though after some little largesse had been pressed into the appropriate palms. On the other side, the Spanish universities naturally stood unanimous for Katherine, while Henry did not even trouble to consult those of Germany. Though his successes had some potential value for his propa-gandists, they failed to stir the Habsburg eagle from its secure nest in the Vatican. The lasting result of the plan lay in the introduction to Henry's notice of the clergyman destined to share with Thomas Cromwell so much of the responsibility for founding a national church in England. In his academic hesi-tancy, his constantly-developing convictions, his literary sense, at once imaginative and precise, his curious blend of pliability and courage, Thomas Cranmer could scarce have presented a greater contrast with the decisive, resolute and practical Crom-well. Yet at every point these two strange midwives of Anglican-ism supplied each other's defects. The harsh logic of history has seldom forced characters so disparate into such complementary roles, but one must not for a moment be tempted to label those roles with the terms 'destructive Cromwell' and 'constructive Cranmer'. The utterly misleading character of such an antithesis will become more apparent as this account advances.

The 'years without a policy' solved few problems, yet they did not lack some notable events. The tension between Church and State mounted amid an atmosphere of foreboding. In 1529 the Reformation Parliament set out along a road the end of which none of its members could have envisaged. It was summoned to deal with a critical situation, and certainly not to stage an ecclesiastical revolution, yet quite empirically, it began to legislate against a few old and obvious abuses. One Act laid down a precise scale of fees to be charged for the probate of wills; another likewise regulated mortuary dues; a third restrained pluralities, forebade clerical trading and debarred beneficed clergy from accepting chantries, the enterprise attacked a century and a half earlier by Chaucer. The fourth of these Acts provided that a criminal taking sanctuary for felony or murder should be branded upon the thumb for future identification, and should lose the benefit of sanctuary if he failed to come forth and abjure the realm on the day appointed by the coroner. These early reforms should also be viewed in conjunction with certain others passed in 1531–2. Ostensibly to prevent able-bodied soldiers and sailors from taking service abroad, one of these later Acts abolished abjuration altogether, confining the criminals to their sanctuaries. Another dealt with the so-called clerics under the lowly order of subdeacon. Should such men be charged with treason, murder, burglary, highway-robbery or arson, they would henceforth forfeit benefit of clergy.

To Gairdner, that paladin of clerical privilege, 'the spirit of the whole legislation was bad, and was clearly intended to punish the only power in the land which could be trusted to denounce wrong in high places with something like authority'. But could it so be trusted? And precisely what moral force derived from the protection of a thug able to stumble through a neck-verse or persuade some incautious bishop to make him an acolyte? Such questions Gairdner does not stop to answer, but he goes on to suggest that these initial reforms could not benefit the poor. If, however, he had studied the scales of probate fees and mortuary dues, he would have seen that in fact they do protect the interests of the poor, and this quite effectively. Then he gives away the game by recalling that these fees had been the subject of complaint in the time of Edward III, but then (when men were sensitive about holy things!) the bishops had merely received notice to amend such abuses.

How long should Parliament and the nation have awaited

these simple reforms? Gairdner might more suitably have reserved his conservative thunders for that other chief episode of the pre-Cromwellian Reformation, the series of events culminating in the Pardon of the Clergy. They began when, in the summer of 1530, writs of *praemunire facias* were issued from the King's Bench against fifteen divines, including eight bishops and three abbots. They were charged with offences under the statutes of *praemunire*, in that they had abetted Wolsey by paying him a portion of their annual revenues. These statutes had culminated in the so-called Great Statute of 1393, the unintentional vagueness of which had left it a formidable if rusty weapon. It had originated in response to the threat of Boniface IX to excommunicate English bishops for implementing obnoxious mandates of the King's courts concerning the patronage of benefices. This Pope had also aroused the wrath of Richard II's Parliament when he threatened to dislocate the work of English government by translating from see to see those bishops who held secular offices. Consequently, the Great Statute had punished with forfeiture of land and goods all persons who should introduce or execute papal bulls injurious to the Crown *in these two particular ways*. It also used high phraseology concerning the independence of the English Crown, 'which hath been so free at all times that it hath been in subjection to no earthly sovereign, but immediately subject to God and no other'. Even so, later attempts to make the Statute exclude *all* papal jurisdiction from the realm lacked historical justification; its text was admittedly ill-drafted and easy to strain, but it neither intended so sweeping an effect nor had made much immediate difference to English practice. After lying dormant for many years, it had been revived by Humphrey Duke of Gloucester as a political weapon against Cardinal Beaufort, while later in the fifteenth century aggressive lay lawyers had used it to stigmatize all ecclesiastical jurisdiction as 'foreign', and had threatened to bring the church courts under the operation of the Great Statute.

The revival of *praemunire* in 1530 and its employment against the fifteen eminent divines obviously sprang from broad political motives. A great many clerics had paid Wolsey these sums, not as an act of submission, but rather to resist him, since, in return for such compositions, the omnipotent Legate could be induced to leave their jurisdictions uncontrolled. 'There is never a poor archdeacon in England', said the Lords in their accusations against Wolsey, 'but that he paid yearly to him a portion of his living.' Several of the defendants may have been selected for this treatment by the government because they had been prominent supporters of Queen Katherine: Fisher of Rochester, West of Ely, Standish of St. Asaph and Clerk of Bath and Wells. Others, however, appear to have supported the King, and seem not to have been chosen on account of governmental rancour. Since some of these men failed to appear in court during the Michaelmas term, a second set of writs summoned them for Hilary term 1531. Before this stage arrived, however, the limited plan was merged into a much larger plan, which involved threatening the whole of the English clergy with a *praemunire* charge. In a message to Wolsey on 21 October, Cromwell himself wrote: 'The prelates shall not appear in the *praemunire*. There is another way devised in place thereof, as your Grace shall further know.' At this moment, Cromwell was about to enter the King's Council, but no evidence can be adduced to prove that it was he who suggested this broadening of the attack.

Quite recently, Mr. Scarisbrick has demonstrated that the new charge against the whole clergy was not, as stated by Hall and consequently by historians ever since, a charge of complicity with Wolsey's usurped jurisdiction. This was merely the accusation against the original fifteen. According to the Act of Pardon subsequently passed, and to other official documents, the charge made against the whole clergy was more sweeping: by merely exercising jurisdiction in their ecclesiastical courts, they had 'fallen and incurred into divers dangers of his [i.e. the King's] laws by things done and perpetrated and committed contrary to the order of his laws and specially contrary to the form of the statutes of provisors, provisions and *praemunire*.' This was a legal fiction of as much crudity as that which had formerly been brought against Wolsey for acting as Papal Legate, though something very similar had long ago been suggested by Crown lawyers. When Convocation met at the end of January 1531, it can scarcely have feared a literal application of the penalties of *praemunire*—loss of property and imprisonment during the King's pleasure—yet it felt justifiable alarm lest its jurisdiction and privileges might suffer arbitrary curtailment by Act of Parliament. Recent debates in the Commons had in fact shown a strong party in favour of such a radical action. Consequently the two Convocations of Canterbury and York agreed without delay to pay the King extraordinary subsidies of £100,000 and £18,840 respectively, in return for a pardon for their alleged offences. The King demanded immediate payment, but the clergy successfully insisted on spreading instalments over five years. They then asked him formally to guarantee their privileges and define the future scope of the *praemunire* act, in order that ecclesiastical judges should know precisely where they stood. It was now Henry's turn to refuse, for the whole advantage of *praemunire* lay in its vagueness: he had everything to lose by stabilizing a situation the very fluidity of which might bring him further sweeping gains.

In February, chief attention turned to a new set of royal demands, two being pre-eminent: that Convocation should acknowledge his sole right to be called 'Protector and Supreme Head of the English Church and Clergy' and that he had the cure of his subjects' souls. The clergy, less subservient during these particular negotiations than has commonly been supposed, refused to agree. They conceded the title of Supreme Head only with the vital saving clause 'so far as the law of Christ allows'; they evaded the royal claim to exercise cure of souls by a clever verbal alteration of the suggested phrase, which rendered it quite innocuous. Altogether, these later attacks did not carry Henry appreciably beyond his previous claims, or indeed beyond the *de facto* powers of previous kings. Here again, the more momentous changes which came after 1532 may well induce us to read into the manoeuvres of 1530–1 more than they were understood at the time to convey. The final plunge had not yet been taken, and ample evidence remains to show that in these years Henry was still hoping against hope for a change of heart in Rome. One can see little more than a formidable campaign of threats intended to remind both the Pope and the English clergy that the King still meant business in the matter of the divorce; this notion makes sense of the somewhat unreal, though not quite unprecedented, crudity of a general attack upon ecclesiastical jurisdiction. The Pardon of the Clergy may thus be regarded as an elaborate essay in brinkmanship rather than a serious first step towards the erection of a national and schismatic Church. Within two years, demands much more precise and irrevocable were to be framed by the Crown and accepted by the English clergy: these demands, not the inconclusive exchanges of 1530–1, mark the entry of Cromwell. Nevertheless, the full length of the front on which the King was prepared to fight now lay revealed. That front covered not merely the whole future of papal jurisdiction and titular headship in England; it covered the independence of the English Church. Irrespective of their attitude towards Rome, the English clergy, their institutions, their jurisdictions, now lay in more danger of legal subjection— whatever in practice that might mean—to the omnicompetent national State.

Within the boundaries of his kingdom, there was little Henry could not accomplish; yet meanwhile in Rome the situation remained static. During the years 1529–32 his advisers lacked any feasible plans either to move the Pope or to dispense altogether with Papal authority. They used one lever after another, and if their levers of 1530–1 were fairly heavy implements, they still lacked the slightest chance of success. By the time of Cromwell's advent, their failure had become all too apparent, and the new minister soon induced the King to abandon the lever in favour of the hammer. Once taken up, the latter instrument rained down its blows with irresistible force; they were timed and placed with great precision, each one just hard enough to achieve its purpose without creating unnecessary havoc. The hammer was statute-law and the striker a Parliament directed by the son of the blacksmith of Putney.

During these same years, the rise of anticlericalism, so far from being restrained by the fall of Wolsey, was fostered by a number of new factors. The burning of Thomas Bilney (a Catholic reformer who held no notable heresies, unless a disbelief in purgatory be so accounted) aroused less excitement than the action of Dr. Parker, chancellor of the Worcester diocese, who in 1531 exhumed and burned the body of a Gloucestershire gentleman for leaving a supposedly heretical will. In this instance laymen had the satisfaction of seeing Parker haled before the King and paying a fine of £300, since no one except the King's officers could legally burn a heretic, dead or alive. It took very few episodes of this type to revive memories of Richard Hunne, since able publicists were now zealously fanning the flames. Chief among these was Christopher St. German, an eminent common lawyer and already in his seventieth year when the Reformation Parliament first met. His theological approach was conservative; in fact, he took little interest in doctrine, the grand passion of his life being the abasement of ecclesiastical jurisdiction. His first book, usually called *Doctor and Student,* had begun its career in 1523 as an academic dialogue in Latin; its more revolutionary suggestions only emerged in 1530–31, when a second dialogue in English was followed by a translation of the first, together with numerous appendices. St. German's other pre-Cromwellian work was his *Division between the Spiritualty and Temporalty,* published in 1532 and inaugurating a famous pamphlet-contest with Sir Thomas More. Then, as the Reformation advanced, the formidable septuagenarian supported it step by step in a further series of writings which acutely discerned its immense implications. His modernity can be overstated, for he drew much upon medieval authors like Marsiglio of Padua, Gerson and Fortescue, yet he grappled with the fundamental problems of law, equity and the relations between Church and State. The claims of St. German are made, not on behalf of any royal despotism, but in favour of a parliamentary absolutism; in several respects this foreshadows the concepts of Cromwell, whom he may well have influenced at a most crucial moment. To the King in Parliament St. German ascribes omnicompetence over all property and temporal things: this mighty organ can control all ecclesiastical exactions, prevent the transfer of land into mortmain, even redistribute property at will between its subjects, clergy and laity alike. Sir Thomas More ridiculed St. German's bland pose as a 'pacifier' in the great controversy, and criticized his habit of reporting dark but unspecific charges against churchmen. But if St. German's tears over clerical sins were hardly sincere, he cannot be blamed for omitting the names, since the bishops would have relished any chance to manhandle so astute an antagonist. St. German admittedly wanted to be in the *avantgarde* and yet avoid the Bishop's consistory court, but More himself was also trying to have it both ways for his episcopal friends. If the latter argued by means of nasty prisons and faggots, they could scarcely expect their opponents to offer them easy chances.

Apart from the fact that its author was also an anticlerical lawyer, Simon Fish's *Supplication for Beggars* has few analogies with the tractates of St. German. Fish was a convinced Protestant making a cruel and wild attack upon the clergy, and exploiting with gross exaggeration the common charges of covetousness and sexual immorality. Though immeasurably their stylistic superior, he surpasses the yellowest elements of the modern press. His pamphlet is couched in the form of a petition by the needy and the sick; they cry out to the King against those holy beggars: bishops, abbots, priests, monks and friars, who have grasped a third of the kingdom's wealth. The Pope is also 'a cruel devilish bloodsupper, drunken with the blood of the saints and martyrs of Christ'; he has held England to ransom since the days of King John. Lured on by their superior wealth, these clergymen corrupt every man's wife, daughter and maid. They have also invented purgatory, that lucrative swindle which enables them to gain money by pretending to release dead souls from pain. No one dare touch them: witness the case of poor Richard Hunne! It is no use founding hospitals for us poor people, since the fat always sticks to the priests' beards. When will the King assert his power, strip away this ill-gotten wealth and force these sturdy lubbers to do some work and keep their own wives? If only this be done, population and wealth will grow, profligacy decrease and the gospel be preached.

Simon Fish was circulating this pamphlet in 1529 and, according to Foxe, Anne Boleyn gave a copy to the King, who kept it in his breast-pocket for several days and protected the author against the wrath of Chancellor More. The story seems over-picturesque, but it does not lack all probability. Although the King must have spotted the cloven hoof of heresy behind these pages, his mood had altered decisively since 1515; in order to marry Anne and have a male heir, he was prepared to use even these savage allies. During the first three years of the Parliament, he came to realize that that there stood behind him not only an anticlerical House of Commons but also, especially in London, an anticlerical public opinion. What he lacked before the year 1532 was a minister with the legal acumen and the resolution to lead these forces towards two clearly-seen objectives: severance from a Roman jurisdiction controlled by his wife's nephew, and the creation of an absolute sovereignty by the Crown in Parliament over all subjects and causes within his realm.

In his work, *The Tudor Revolution in Government*, Dr. Elton has made a detailed survey of the offices held by Cromwell and the use he made of them during the great changes, which, from another angle, we are about to observe. Here a very few salient features will suffice. He began in 1532–3 with three appointments—Master of the King's Jewels, Clerk of the Hanaper and Chancellor of the Exchequer—each then relatively unimportant, but together enabling him to begin the rehabilitation of

Crown finances, a task obviously connected with several aspects of his ecclesiastical policy. In 1534 he became Principal Secretary and Master of the Rolls: it was the secretaryship which mattered, for he proceeded to take it out of its Household context and to set the future pattern by making it a ministry of all affairs. There was henceforth no aspect of Crown administration which he could not and did not touch: in particular his active personal role in the drafting of parliamentary legislation is amply attested in the records. In 1535, Cromwell became Vicegerent in Spirituals: a new and curious minister for Church-affairs. The following year he was appointed Lord Privy Seal and a baron.

As will become all too obvious, Henrician ministers were totally dependent upon the King's personal favour and, however capricious or mistaken Henry might be, the least puff of his displeasure could bring down his mightiest servant. And in relation to ecclesiastical matters, it should from the first be recognized that Cromwell's situation always contained elements of grave weakness. He adhered to one of two schools of thought which arose from the Royal Supremacy: the one which soon proved to have the less secure hold upon Henry's doctrinal sympathies. This Reforming group, led by Cranmer and Cromwell, numbered amongst its members Nicholas Shaxton, Bishop of Salisbury, Hugh Latimer, Bishop of Worcester, and William Barlow, Bishop of St. Asaph and St. Davids. Their theology was in considerable measure Lutheran and never liked by the King, who, having used them to help establish his Supremacy, broke their influence in the reaction of 1539-40. Cranmer apart, the small knot of Reforming bishops and their clerical supporters afforded Cromwell little support; not infrequently they caused him embarrassment. Men like Shaxton and Latimer had all the faults of the academic zealot, while moderate Reformers combining zeal with tact and worldly wisdom failed to emerge. Cranmer alone proved an asset on account of his unique relationship with the King. 'You were born', Cromwell told him, 'in a happy hour, I suppose, for, do or say what you will, the King will always well take it at your hand.' Yet in the longer run, even this influence proved a broken reed; at a moment of crisis Cranmer never managed to protect anything or anyone else from the Wrath of the Prince, which, in a favourite political proverb of the age, was Death.

51

Chapter Four

The Erastian Revolution

THE statutes which revolutionized both Anglo-Papal and Church-State relations admittedly lack the charm of novelty, yet no aspect of Cromwell's work illustrates to better effect his organizing genius, his grasp of detail, his ability to clinch an issue. Considering their extent, they give rise to few interpretative problems. They were drafted under his close personal supervision and, despite a weakness for grandiloquent preambles which caused one adversary to call them whited sepulchres, he was capable of making his intentions admirably clear.

The initial year 1532 did not show an instant change of method; Cromwell was no doubt concerting his plans and winning over the King and others to full participation. Nevertheless, the destruction of the English Church's legal independence was carried one stage nearer completion. On 18 March the Supplication of the Commons against the Ordinaries, originally drafted by Cromwell himself in 1529, was presented to the King in a revised form. Having admittedly begun its career as a Commons document, did the Supplication derive in 1532 from a still active fund of animosity in the House, or had it now become essentially a 'government measure'? Much rigorous analysis has recently been applied to its extant drafts, yet with divergent results; some aspects of this excessively involved problem still lie *sub judice*, but one may well remain sceptical as to the possibility of any unambiguous verdict. It seems, however, apparent that Cromwell continued in 1532 at least to help draft the Commons' ecclesiastical grievances and that, for their part, the Commons continued to display genuine indignation against the bishops' conduct of heresy-cases at least as late as 1534. The measure was also reintroduced by its sponsors at a moment when the House, irritated by financial demands and by the bills of Wills and Uses, could easily be turned against the Church. The Supplication ascribed the discords of the realm to heretical opinions and to 'the extreme and uncharitable behaviour and dealing of divers ordinaries, who have the right to examine these heresies'. It proceeded thence to enumerate 'certain particular griefs': the power of Convocation to legislate without the assent of King and laity; the vexatious delays and exactions of the church courts; the bestowal of benefices by nepotists upon minors, whereby the poor silly souls of the King's subjects perish for lack of instruction; the excessive number of holy days kept, and 'with small devotion'; the trapping of alleged lay heretics through 'subtle interrogatories concerning the high mysteries of our faith'. This was a cleverly variegated display: on the one hand a justified criticism of abuses, on the other a radical attack upon Convocation's legislative status. The reply of the bishops, probably drafted by Gardiner, was lengthy and less astute. It argued that the Commons grossly exaggerated the discords and that, if those things were really happening, they sprang from the faults of individuals rather than from the system. Where good cause could be shown, reform would be forthcoming, yet the independent legislative power of the clergy had a divine origin, and could not be surrendered. To submit the making of canon laws to the royal assent was beyond the power of the ordinaries. 'We your most humble subjects may not submit the execution of our charge and duty, certainly prescribed by God, to your Highness's assent.'

Henry transmitted the answer of the bishops to the Commons along with the heaviest of hints. 'We think their answer will smally please you, for it seemeth to us very slender. You be a great sort of wise men; I doubt not but you will look circumspectly on the matter, and we shall be indifferent between you.' Had the clergy passionately believed in their legislative independence, they would have resisted at this last ditch, but such convictions as they possessed proved insufficient to disturb their ingrained habit of temporizing with the Crown. Once they knew the King's mind, they offered to delay the operation of new canons pending his approval, and even to revoke old canons found contrary to the laws of the realm, always provided these canons did not touch faith and morals. But the King and his advisers now saw they could play for higher stakes. On 10 May they sent Convocation three articles for its acceptance: that it should pass no new canons unless the King should license it to do so, and supply his assent; that it should submit all canons previously enacted to the King and a commission of 32 clerics and laymen; and that canons thought by a majority of this commission to be repugnant to the laws of God and of the realm should be abrogated, the rest to stand in full power once they received the royal authority. These articles were rapidly followed by a skilful touch of indirect menace. The next day the King sent for the Speaker and twelve of the Commons; to them he explained in plain langugage that he had once thought the clergy wholly his subjects, but now he perceived them to be but half his subjects, since the prelates at their consecration made an oath to the Pope clean contrary to their oath to himself. In modern terms, the long-tolerated division of loyalties seemed to him incompatible with the absolute sovereignty claimed for the State. Precisely what deliberations preceded this meeting we do not know, but Cromwell was supposed by Pole, Foxe and others to have put such ideas into Henry's head. Since the new minister repeatedly expressed similar concepts, he may reasonably be credited with an active and perhaps dominant part in formulating these vital demands, which came so perilously near to abolishing the ancient legislative independence of the Church in England. Nevertheless, could the King have foreseen this as a half-way house towards a lay society liberated altogether from ecclesiastical laws, he would no doubt have experienced profound dismay. This more radical concept lay well outside Tudor possibilities, but if Thomas Cromwell ever envisaged it, one may suspect that he would have been far less shocked than his conventional sovereign. In the event, the Henrician Reformation never looked like taking this second step: ecclesiastical courts and laws continued their losing battle to supervise the nation's faith and morals into and beyond the next century.

Faced by the peremptory royal articles and the menacing talk of the King, the clergy capitulated, and on 16 May they presented him with the document known as the Submission of the Clergy, which granted his demands. And with a fine sense of occasion, Sir Thomas More the next day resigned the Chancellorship, being succeeded by Cromwell's friend Audley.

On the papal front, the year 1532 produced conflicts far less radical and dramatic, but it contributed one enactment of importance, the Conditional Restraint of Annates, which (to revert to our former distinction) falls into the class of levers rather than hammers. Annates were the payments to the Pope for the first year's revenues of bishops, a hoary exaction long resented and under dispute four years previously. The act of 1532 preserved a mild tone: it still spoke respectfully of the Pope, reasserted the Catholic state of the realm, and envisaged the continued appointment of bishops by papal bull. It had two aims. It threatened to deprive Rome of annates, should negotiations to abolish them fail. Equally important, it stipulated that bishops might be consecrated by English authority if the Pope refused bulls of consecration. The immediate purpose of these threats became apparent early the following year, when, with the see of Canterbury at long last vacant by the death of Warham, Henry promoted Thomas Cranmer. Aided by such legislation and by French pressure upon the Pope, he had no difficulty in procuring for his nominee the necessary bulls of consecration.

By this time, however, the moment of revolution was at hand. Of all the Reformation acts, that in Restraint of Appeals, passed in February–March 1533, was at once the most epoch-making, the most clear in its statement of principles, the most central to the Henrician Reformation. It was the banner in Cromwell's hand when he led the nation across the Rubicon. Its immediate purpose may nevertheless be described in terms far less magniloquent: it aimed to free Henry for remarriage, and it is obviously connected with the fact that Anne Boleyn gave birth to the Princess Elizabeth on 7 September, 1533, having been secretly married to Henry in the previous January. It begins with a famous principle obviously borrowed from that fourteenth-century apostle of erastianism, Marsiglio of Padua. England is an Empire, a realm the ruler of which acknowledges no superior human power, governed by one Supreme Head, to whom both spiritual and temporal men are bound to bear next to God a natural and humble obedience. By divine sufferance, the King is endowed with plenary power to give justice to all his people in all causes, without restraint or provocation to any foreign princes or potentates. As for the spiritualty or Church of England, they have always been reputed of sufficient learning and authority to settle matters of divine law without the meddling of any exterior person. Whereas the English Kings, especially Edward I, Edward III, Richard II and Henry IV, made laws to preserve the prerogatives of the imperial crown, and to keep it from the annoyance of the see of Rome and other foreign potentates, nevertheless appeals to Rome in cases of matrimony, testaments, tithes and the like have caused the King and his subjects much vexation and cost, while the great delays resulting from such appeals to this distant tribunal have left the suitors without remedy. Henceforth all these cases shall finally be adjudged within the realm, appeals being carried from the archdeacon to the bishop, and from the bishop to the archbishop, save in matters touching the King, where appeals shall go directly to the Upper House of Convocation.

The successive drafts of this important statute have been submitted to close analysis by Dr. Elton, and with some interesting results. Cromwell emerges throughout as the dominant personality; his clerks drew up most of these drafts, while he personally added some of the most important clauses and constantly corrected others. The theory of the preamble was that set forth under Marsilian inspiration by Cromwell and his pamphleteers. He also called a conference of expert clergy to approve the text before it went to Parliament, and initially he made some concession to clerical views on the course of appeals, for the clergy had a natural anxiety lest the higher ecclesiastical courts should be excluded from this field of business. Once in Parliament, however, Cromwell gained his essential points: he ensured that causes affecting the King should not be dragged through a succession of courts, but go straight to Convocation. And, as will appear, in a later Act he gave ordinary suitors an appeal even beyond the courts of the Archbishop. In general, Cromwell's drafting tended towards the elimination of moral platitudes and towards the stressing of concrete abuses likely to impress Parliament. He also appears to have prevailed upon the King to allow the removal of merely apologetic passages and of uneasy protestations against possible charges of heresy. He had no use for such qualms, such sensitivities which might betray a lack of confidence. So far as can be seen from personal corrections, Henry's direct responsibility for the drafting remained small: at one stage he indeed asserted the high claim that both the temporal and the spiritual jurisdictions in England proceeded 'from the said imperial Crown and none otherwise', but this phrase was not in fact retained. From first to last, the Appeals Act was a government measure, and in the Commons it encountered considerable opposition during the fortnight which followed its first reading on 14 March 1533. Yet according to Chapuys, this resistance was based upon mundane grounds: upon the fear that the Pope might induce other nations to ruin England by refusing to trade with a nation of schismatics. In the event, the bill passed Parliament with only one amendment of substance: that which Henry and Cromwell desired and which affected the course of appeals in the King's cases. The passage of the Act marked the complete winning of the King's confidence by Cromwell, who in the following month was openly acknowleged to be the chief minister of the Crown.

The effectiveness of this Act in relation to the immediate problem of the royal divorce found speedy illustration. In April and May both Convocations were induced to declare that it was against the law of God, and not dispensable even by the Pope, for a man to marry his brother's widow when her previous marriage had been consummated; again, that the consummation of Katherine's marriage with Arthur had been sufficiently proved. A few members of both Convocations ventured to vote against the propositions, but they were carried by heavy majorities. In all these changes, the Convocation of York did not show more signs of resistance than that of Canterbury. The attribution of superior toughness to the northern clerical proctors springs partly from Froude's imagination, partly from the misdating of Bishop Tunstall's protest against the Royal Supremacy, and the false attribution of this personal protest to the whole Convocation of York. At York, as in the Southern Province, the representatives of the clergy were safe, elderly and eminent. Both Convocations were handled by Cromwell's emissaries with tact and skill.

It is a fact of immense significance that some of the ablest clergy in the country had already ranged themselves on his side, and were doing his bidding with zeal and efficiency. On this occasion of the divorce debates, for example, the Dean of York and Archdeacon Magnus (a former diplomat and now a phenomenal pluralist) were reinforced by Dr. Rowland Lee, then Archdeacon of Cornwall, King's chaplain, Master in Chancery and Bishop-elect of Chester. Lee's subsequent letter to Cromwell admirably depicts the lobbying by which Tudor governments furthered their will in Convocation. He first had two lengthy interviews with Tunstall, the leader of the northern conservatives. When Tunstall excused himself, as a former counsel of Queen Katherine, from openly maintaining the King's case, Rowland Lee was not a little shocked. 'I am sorry to see so little stay towards the Prince's, our master's, honour by such. It is no marvel [if] strangers shall strangely censure, when we ourselves so do by him by whom we be supported, specially the thing now done. Thus I write you secretly. Would God we were of one mind, but the diversities of minds in ourselves shall hurt us.' This clerical royalist, sustained by a 'most loving letter' from Cromwell, then arranged for conferences between Dr. Edward Leghton, an Oxford scholar in the King's service, and the hesitant Archdeacon of Nottingham, who had offered to be tractable if he could be convinced by scholarship. Then Lee turned to the chief figures among the northern monks. 'The Abbot of Fountains, I trust, will be good. Now I am towards Byland, Newburgh and Rievaulx. The Abbot of Welbeck will not fail to do the best he can. The Abbot of St. Mary's also, but he is not learned. There shall be as much done as I may.' Here we may see an example of the methods by which the Cromwellian proposals so smoothly traversed the organs of Church and State. We should be wise to think rather less of the dictator with the mailed fist, rather more of the campaign-manager supported by a small but devoted band of constituency-workers. The Restraint of Appeals and the propositions in Convocation ended the legal resistance of Queen Katherine, for Cromwell had now stopped all the loopholes open to her counsel. The facts of the case were prejudged and her appeal to Rome was positively debarred. When Cranmer was licensed by the King to hear the suit, she naturally refused his summons to appear, and on 23 May he declared her marriage *ab initio* null and void.

While the parliamentary session of 1533 thus saw the final severance of the papal nexus and the arrangement of the divorce, the two sessions of 1534 produced a rush of Cromwellian legislation to complete the massive structure of the Royal Supremacy. That of January–March was signalized by four important statutes. The Act in Restraint of Annates covers much more than its title would imply. Besides making absolute the former conditional restraint of annates, it also forbids the procurement from Rome of bulls, briefs, palls, or other things requisite for archbishops and bishops. Moreover, bishops must henceforth be elected by cathedral chapters on receipt of the royal *congé d'élire*, this document being accompanied by letters missive nominating the person chosen by the King. Any member of a chapter who failed to comply became liable to the penalties of *praemunire*, while in the event of a delay of twelve days the King could appoint by letters patent. Under the same penalties, the archbishop must proceed to consecrate. It was in correct interpretation of this act that Lord John Russell wrote in 1848 to a canon of Hereford, who had said he could not conscientiously vote for Queen Victoria's nominee, 'Sir, I have the honour to acknowledge your letter of the 20th instant in which you announce your intention of breaking the law'. At the same time, this dramatic illustration of erastianism did little more than give statutory sanction to the royal control *de facto* operative even at medieval episcopal elections.

The Dispensations Act began by cutting off all payments to Rome, including Peter's pence, the ancient tribute said to date from the time of King Offa, but since the twelfth century commuted by the bishops for a mere £200 per annum. The main purpose of the act was to ensure that dispensations, faculties and other sorts of licences, no longer obtainable from Rome, should be issued by the Archbishop of Canterbury under Crown supervision. This was no academic matter, but one of daily administrative practice. Dispensations were licences either giving authority for some act otherwise illegal in canon law, or remitting the penalty for a breach. In later medieval times they had become largely a papal prerogative; they had in fact occasioned great delays and expenses, as they applied to a wide field of transactions, such as matrimony, ordination, vows, and the translation of bishops from one see to another. In transferring the power to grant such licences to the Archbishop, Cromwell was careful to forestall the possibility that the Canterbury registry might reproduce in miniature the administrative shortcomings of the papal Curia. If henceforth the Archbishop should fail to provide a dispensation upon a reasonable claim, then the Lord Chancellor would direct the King's writ to him, enjoining him under penalty to grant the dispensation, or else to explain his refusal by a certain day to the King in Chancery. This interesting statute also disclaims any intention by the King and his subjects 'to decline or vary from the congregation of Christ's Church in any things concerning the very articles of the Catholic faith of Christendom, or in any other things declared by Holy Scripture and the word of God necessary for your (i.e. the King's) and their salvations, but only to make an ordinance by policies necessary and convenient to repress vice, and for good conservation of this realm in peace, unity and tranquillity, from ravin and spoil'. It ends with the proviso that those religious houses formerly exempt from visitation by the English bishops should not now be transferred to the latter, but should instead be visited by royal commissioners. It forms in short the monument of a layman who boldly identified efficiency with lay control.

The third of these important enactments was the Act for Submission of the Clergy, which put into the statute book the promises given by the Convocations in 1532. It still retains practical force, in that it prohibits Convocation from legislating except by licence of the Crown and with subsequent royal assent—a provision recently invoked to demonstrate the illegality of regulations made by Convocation in 1957 concerning marriage and divorce. The Submission Act also brought Parliament into the foreground, with its obvious implication that the King in Parliament bore an authority superior to that of the King in Convocation. Since Henry in his egotism and theological knowledge took a dangerously personal view of his ecclesiastical supremacy, the Church of England may well owe this element of institutionalism to Cromwell. Fortunately also, Henry's successors were a minor and two women, none of them able and disposed to attempt a quasi-papal role in their own persons. In this broadening of the basis of the Supremacy, Convocation was assigned little part, for Cromwell had every intention of ensuring its subjection to parliamentary controls. Convocation henceforth lacked importance, not merely in English history but in English ecclesiastical history. A further clause of the Submission Act modified the Act of Appeals by providing for a final appeal beyond the Archbishop to the King in Chancery, who would appoint special commissioners, called a Court of Delegates, for each case as it arose.

Finally in this series, the first Succession Act vested the succession to the Crown in the heirs of Henry and Anne, making it high treason to slander the marriage, as many people were doing, or to question the succession 'by writing, print, deed or act'. The spacious generalities of this statute now form an amusing example of royal propaganda, yet its rehearsal of the horrors attendant upon disputed successions do not lack a bitter historical justification; no thoughtful subject of Henry VIII, whatever his creed, can lightly have dismissed such a possibility. Parliament is made to call to its remembrance 'the great divisions which in times past had been in the realm by reason of several titles pretended to the imperial Crown of the same'; when ambiguities allowed 'that men might upon intents expound them to every man's sinister appetite and affection . . . whereof hath ensued great effusion and destruction of man's blood'. Parliament also recalled 'that the good unity, peace and wealth of this realm . . . most specially and principally above all worldly things consisteth and resteth in the certainty and surety of the procreation and posterity of your Highness'. In these terms Cromwell gauged accurately enough the prevalent sense of the nation, the reasoning which, despite the unpopularity of the divorce, carried the people through the crisis behind their ruler. This mood was realistic: any marriage, any undisputed heir, any legal continuity seemed better than the prospect of the abyss. During the century of so-called religious wars, the English nation looked after itself much more effectively than did the French or the Germans. Behind the welter of theological and philosophical rationalization, this instinct for cohesion and social survival must surely be regarded as the recurrent *leit-motif* of the whole Tudor age.

Cromwell saw to it that the Succession Act was far more than a declaration, far more even than a threat. He included a clause to the effect that every subject of full age should take an oath to defend and observe the act. Though he cannot have planned to swear in a whole nation, he soon showed every intention of applying this acid test to eminent or potentially dangerous people. For their refusal to take this oath Sir Thomas More and Bishop Fisher went to the Tower; they accepted that part which acknowledged the right of Parliament to settle the succession upon the heirs of Anne Boleyn, but rejected the parts touching the Royal Supremacy and the unlawfulness of the King's first marriage. The story of their interrogation, imprisonment, trial and ultimate executions (June–July 1535) is marked by a very human heroism, by a cheerful acceptance, by a certain spiritual distinction which make it difficult to subject their standpoints to cold analysis. There are nevertheless some important differences between Fisher and More. In the conduct of the former there was without doubt an element of active disloyalty, justified or unjustified, towards the Crown.

The King already bore Fisher a grudge for his bold championship of Katherine and for his sympathy with the false prophecies of the Nun of Kent. This unfortunate servant-girl had been exploited by a foolish knot of ecclesiastics and taken seriously by many eminent people. By 1533 her utterances turned political to the point of threatening the King with death if he remarried. Moreover, her clerical backers circulated books concerning her revelations and planned to print them. The mildest government could not have allowed the escapade to continue, for political prophecies had always played an important part in sedition and rebellion; they were shortly to have a very large share in provoking the Pilgrimage of Grace. Though More had been relatively discreet, Fisher had on his own admission personally listened to revelations about the King's death, had thought them to be 'threats of God' and failed to report them. A long letter from Cromwell to Fisher rebuts the excuses offered by the Bishop, and urges him to avoid the real risks which in the course of a trial his admissions would present, and frankly to confess his fault to the King. There is nothing sinister about this letter; indeed, it demonstrates that if Cromwell had none of Fisher's holiness, his upbringing had at least emancipated him from such dangerous nonsense. In the end, Fisher was lucky to have his sentence commuted by the angry King to a heavy fine.

If about this same time Henry could have read the correspondence between Chapuys and the Emperor Charles V, his anger would already have reached boiling-point, since Fisher was joining in frequent clandestine conferences with the Imperial ambassador, during which the two concerted measures to thwart the royal policy. Of one such parley Chapuys writes to Charles: 'I see no appearance of these people preparing to yield to the papal censures . . . for as that excellent and holy man the bishop of Rochester told me some time ago, the Pope's weapons become very malleable when directed against the obdurate and pertinacious, and therefore it is incumbent upon your Majesty to interfere in this affair and undertake a work which must be as pleasing in the eyes of God as war upon the Turk.' Chapuys then propounds a plan whereby Reginald Pole should be put upon the throne, though he does not also ascribe the suggestion to Fisher. This was written on 27 September, 1533, and on 10 October, in another secret letter to Charles, the ambassador relates that Bishop Fisher 'advises prompt action on the part of your Majesty, such as I recommended in one of my last despatches. Indeed, not many days ago he sent me word to say that strong measures must now be taken. In the opinion of this good and pious bishop, the majority of the English nation, as I am told, concur; no one doubts but that your Majesty will take the affair in hand.'

Commenting on these passages, Fisher's recent Catholic biographer has written that the Bishop would not have taken this extreme view unless he felt in conscience compelled so to do. 'In his day such an attitude would not seem as disaffected as it would today. Violent changes in dynasties had occurred in his childhood, and the Wars of the Roses were a living memory; the medieval idea that the Emperor of the Holy Roman Empire was the ordained temporal power had been weakened, but it was not completely lifeless.' This is a commendably frank admission, yet we remain at liberty to doubt whether even Fisher framed his actions upon so antiquated a notion as the legality of armed Imperial intervention in the affairs of European kingdoms. In both the good and the bad senses, Fisher had indeed old-fashioned notions, but it is not easy to assign him a role which had seemed antediluvian even in the time of Dante. Whatever be the case, this odd situation *vis à vis* Fisher surely illustrates the strength of the Cromwellian thesis. When a man of such gifts could think about politics as Fisher did; when a Spanish invasion, a civil war, a deposition, and perhaps a Yorkist pretender, were envisaged as the means to save the nation from schism, it was no time to be casual and easygoing. A minister must be prepared either to see all these things happen, or else to strike hard at those who planned them. Fisher could make no pretences to being either a politician or a political prophet, but the imperceptiveness of Chapuys now seems even grosser. His picture of a nation of ardent papalists anxiously awaiting a lead to hurl their heretical rulers from power: this was to become the common dream of Spanish ambassadors and of English *émigrés* for many a long day. And there are writers who still think it true!

Thomas More has been too readily paired off with John Fisher. The ten years' gap between their ages, the marked divergence of their professions and intellectual activities had caused them to approach some of the basic problems from very different angles. More's memory did not hark back to the Wars of the Roses; he had been a child when the first Tudor came to the throne. He was not a theologian of international reputation, but a common lawyer and a great servant of the Crown. He understood the noble aims and solid achievements of the dynasty; in large measure he accepted the rising claims of the State; he parted only with the utmost reluctance from the path upon which Cromwell strove to hold him. If he displayed a shrewd appreciation of Henry's weaknesses, he shared with the rest of Henrician officialdom a reverence for the person of the King as well as a theoretical loyalty to the Crown. Above all, he was not, like most of the prominent oppositionists, a secret frequenter of the Imperial embassy. He had no sympathies with foreign-directed conspiracy, with aristocratic rebellions, with that complex of backward-looking causes, which inevitably exploited and thereby limited the appeal of papalism to Englishmen. On his own showing, his feeling for the Roman primacy had in early life been weak; he claimed—and so solemn a claim cannot in his mouth be regarded as sarcasm—to have been reconverted to this primacy by reading the King's own book written against Luther. Since Henry's change of outlook, More had tried his best by reading and discussion to see the royal case. He offered to swear to the Boleyn succession if he might be released from acknowledging the abolition of papal authority in England. He agreed to accept as heir to the throne anyone Parliament might choose; even Elizabeth, who had been declared illegitimate by the Pope.

Yet while More came near to sharing Cromwell's high view of the omnicompetence of an English Parliament, he felt in the last resort bound to regard it as inferior to the faith of earlier generations, to the laws of the Church, to the accepted tenets of foreign Christian countries. His loud praise of General Councils looked backward to Constance rather than forward to Trent; it seems far from identical with the new papalism of the thirties. On the other hand, his assertion that he had France on his side seemed 'rank malice' to the Duke of Norfolk and many other Englishmen, for France was still the traditional enemy. His recorded utterances make him a clearer martyr for the idea of international Christendom than for that of papal monarchy in the Church. When, however, he took his stand on the unity of Christendom, he passed completely beyond the things which a mind like that of Thomas Cromwell could accept as realities. While acknowledging the grave imperfections of the Church on earth, he yet accorded it his allegiance as a supranational authority in spiritual causes. When at his trial More at last gave up lawyerly attempts to save himself, those in Westminster Hall heard the challenge well and truly made. 'This realm, being but one member and small part of the Church, might not make a particular law dischargeable with the general law of Christ's holy Catholic Church, no more than the City of London, being but one poor member in respect of the whole realm, might make a law against an act of Parliament'. And when the Chancellor asked him if he would be considered wiser and of better conscience than all the bishops and nobles, More answered, 'I am not bounden, my Lord, to conform my conscience to the Council of one realm against the General Council of Christendom. For of the foresaid holy bishops I have, for every bishop of yours, above one hundred; and for one Council or Parliament of yours (God knoweth what manner of one), I have all the Councils made these thousand years. And for this one kingdom, I have all other Christian realms.'

Here was conservatism in its most broad-minded, its most responsible, its most attractive form, yet we may well question the extent to which it could be imposed upon the far less attractive facts of sixteenth-century history. When we pass beyond the strictly theological problems, More's case has obvious weaknesses. Some French Catholic scholars show obvious impatience at this supposed spectacle of heretical England diverging from a United Catholic Europe into an obstinate political and cultural insularity. Few Englishmen of any creed can see this as a true summary of the facts. In the first place, most of northern Europe was diverging and Spain, not England, looks to us the dangerous eccentric of the European family. Had More lived as a nonagenarian to see the Revolt of the Netherlands, whose side would he then have taken? Were Englishmen morally bound to belong to a club, the papal chairman of which was ordered in political and even politico-religious matters by the mighty Habsburg combination, by the famed Spanish infantry, by the Spanish monopoly of Mexican and Peruvian silver? And how could Spain's hold over Rome be shattered, save by transferring it to the older enemy, France? Were rulers like Philip II scrupulous to keep political and religious controls apart? Has not England performed notable services for Europe by resolutely refusing to join all those national hegemonies which have worn the sheep's clothing of international creeds? Had either Fisher or More the least inkling of the way Europe was going, or of the harsh influences which politics were to impose upon religion during the years which lay ahead? What of More's proposition, 'as London's law is to England's, so England's law is to that of Christendom'? How much sense did this make as the century developed? These are not theological questions, but they are questions of broader purport which historians need to ask themselves and others, lest the rousing spectacle of More at his trial may induce the unwary to envisage a far-sighted internationalist confronting a myopic, nationalist and insular Cromwell. If the issues of the sixteenth century were as simple as this, the tasks of its historians could be limited to mere factual research.

In examining these august offenders Cromwell did not, as M. Constant asserts, submit them to needless mental cruelty. He merely performed the functions of a Tudor minister. Extremely little personal bitterness existed between him and More. That during the period of the examinations Cromwell could be both helpful and distressed, we have More's own clear testimony. In a letter to Margaret Roper written from the Tower, More says that when he offered with the King's licence to give his reasons for refusing to answer, Cromwell pointed out to him the legal dangers of·this course. 'In this good warning, he showed himself my especial tender friend.' Just as pointedly, More relates that on his final refusal of the oath, Cromwell 'said and sware a great oath, that he had liever that his own son (which is of truth a goodly young gentleman, and shall I trust come to much worship) had lost his head, than that I should thus have refused the oath'. It is an amusing example of M. Constant's handling of Cromwell that he cuts down this quotation to the phrase 'said and sware a great oath', omitting the rest and thus making Cromwell guilty of profanity instead ·of compassion! And so far as the treatment of the two prisoners is concerned, it was Anthony Bonvisi, an intimate friend of Cromwell, who regularly sent them delicacies, a thing hardly possible if Cromwell were deliberately subjecting them to harsh treatment.

In general it is agreed, even by unfavourable critics like Merriman, that Cromwell did not display that revengeful or passionate attitude towards opponents which so often marked the behaviour of the King. It was the latter who refused Cranmer's merciful suggestion that Fisher and More should be allowed to take a modified oath in accordance with their scruples; when M. Constant says that here Henry was 'influenced possibly by Anne Boleyn and Cromwell', he is simply indulging in unwarranted speculation. And when Rome inadvisedly raised Fisher to the cardinalate, it was Henry's wrath which sealed the fate of the prisoners. If Cromwell had little in common with Fisher, he knew More well. United by devotion to the sovereign, divided by their attitudes towards the international Church, both were fully conscious of the issues at stake, and had apparently been over them together in previous times. But for the indolence of More's biographer Harpsfield, the clash might have been far more graphically illustrated in the extant record. Harpsfield became well acquainted with their common friend Bonvisi, who, says Harpsfield, would often talk of More 'and also of Sir Thomas Cromwell, with whom he was many years familiarly acquainted, and would report many notable and as yet commonly unknown things and of their unlike natures, dispositions, sayings and doings, whereof there is now no place to talk'. There he infuriatingly leaves the matter, and every lover of history will echo the comment of More's modern biographer that Harpsfield almost deserved his sixteen years in the Fleet prison for leaving untold the tempers of these mighty opposites, as related by an intelligent observer with a unique knowledge of both.

Meanwhile, a week before the end of the first parliamentary session of 1534, the Pope had given sentence in favour of Queen Katherine. While fireworks and salvoes of cannon greeted this belated triumph of papal justice, the Roman crowds shouted 'Empire and Spain'. 'Other victories', wrote a simple-minded correspondent of the Emperor, 'have been gained over men; this one is over enemies let loose from hell.' Yet from the viewpoint of Cromwell, the gesture could not have been better timed, for it cemented his work beyond any likelihood of collapse. Unsatisfied, however, with these already remarkable legislative achievements, he elaborated throughout the summer and autumn of 1534 the top floors of the building : three more statutes passed in the session of November–December and leaving the legal edifice of the Henrician Reformation virtually complete.

To the Act of Supremacy the metaphor 'ornamental copingstone' has understandably been applied. It does not confer the Supreme Headship, but merely recognizes it as already existent; it also assigns to the Crown the power of ecclesiastical visitation. The limiting-clause, 'so far as the law of Christ allows', is now dropped. The King has assumed the juridical powers and even, by a species of remote-control, certain of the spiritual powers formerly enjoyed in England by the Papacy. The efforts of Henrician publicists to supply theological and philosophical theories of the Royal Supremacy will soon occupy our attention, yet it must immediately be recognized that Henry, Cromwell and Parliament envisaged a Supremacy passing well beyond mere judicial and financial controls. It is true that Henry never asserted a right to administer the sacraments; he did not proclaim himself the personal originator of doctrine; he did not personally preach sermons. Even so, his bishops could not enunciate doctrines or frame liturgies except by his approbation; if he disliked a preacher's opinions, he did not scruple to correct them in public. Even in 1531, he had claimed to be head over the spiritual men of his realm and all their acts, denying any rigid boundaries between *spiritualia* and *temporalia*. In later years he spoke of himself as having committed to him the care of his subjects' souls and bodies. Some Henrician theologians told the King that he could appoint and depose bishops at will. Certainly he soon claimed to administer and confiscate ecclesiastical properties, to reform the canon law, to control ecclesiastical legislation, to try heretics in person and, above all, to visit and discipline the clergy, both regular and secular. At this moment, Henry and Cromwell did not stop to define and thereby to circumscribe the Royal Supremacy by precise definitions. They were more intent to prepare for the next steps. The sting in the tail of the Supremacy Act lay in that mention of visitatorial powers which heralded the dissolution of the smaller monasteries, a process by now certainly envisaged.

Only the simpler of the unfortunate clergy can have supposed that their liberation from the financial exactions of Rome would make them richer. If any were so optimistic, their minds must speedily have been clarified when they perused the Act annexing first-fruits and tenths to the Crown. The conditional restraint of annates had denounced first-fruits as 'intolerable and importable', an almost unique display of incaution in Cromwellian drafting, since the plan to transfer them wholesale and much augmented to the Crown must now involve a measure of embarrassment. Cromwell and his assistants made the best of a bad job and unblushingly launched upon a new preamble of high stylistic quality. In somewhat involved yet mellifluous phrases, it dwells upon the love of a faithful nation for its dread, benign and gracious sovereign lord, 'in whom dwelleth all their joy and weal', its gratitude for the manner in which he has maintained peace and unity, the great, excessive and inestimable charges he has sustained, and so to the inexorable deduction: that he should enjoy, not only the first year's revenue of every ecclesiastical benefice, but also a 'yearly rent or pension' amounting to one-tenth of all its profits, spiritual and temporal. To execute this statute Cromwell prepared in 1535 one of the most technically accomplished of his administrative programmes: that his was the directing mind can readily be seen from the streams of correspondence between him and the commissioners he appointed in each diocese. They were charged to establish the gross income of every ecclesiastical benefice and corporation; alongside this they must place allowances (*allocationes*) such as annual rent-charges, synodals, regular alms distributed under the wills of benefactors, fees of stewards, bailiffs, auditors and receivers. After the deduction of these allowances, the Crown was entitled to the net remainder of one year's income as first-fruits, and thenceforward annually to one-tenth of this remainder. Each incumbent was to pay his annual tenth by Christmas, each bishop to collect the tax for his diocese and transmit it to the Crown by 1 April in the following year.

The commissions themselves are dated 30 January, 1535. Detailed instructions accompanied them showing how the commissioners should divide into sub-commissions, each to its group of rural deaneries, how they should examine incumbents and other officials under oath, inspect registers and account-books. The precise forms to be taken by their returns were also minutely specified. They must miss no sort of benefice, but include episcopal sees, cathedrals, archdeaconries, rural deaneries, colleges, hospitals, monasteries, rectories, vicarages and chapels. In each case, the names of the manors, farms, tenants and other sources of revenue must appear; also the names of the officials whose fees counted as allowances. For the same purpose they took the names of any recipients of rents and pensions, even those of donors for the benefit of whose souls alms had been endowed. Many of these amateur commissioners of inland revenue inevitably plied Cromwell with queries about doubtful cases; he had even to settle quarrels over precedence as between the commissioners themselves. Naturally the chief task was to prevent the taxpayers from submitting underestimates of income, a difficult business, since tithes were paid in kind and a little mild collusion between incumbents and their parishioners could greatly diminish the figures. Cromwell and his henchmen did their best to prevent such evasions. They even ensured that the bishop, though usually chairman of his diocesan commission, should be the only ecclesiastic upon it, since clerical sympathies might lie on the side of the payers. The rest were mayors, sheriffs, justices of the peace, local gentry and professional auditors, all men unlikely to be restrained by excessive tenderness. In the event, the bishops strove like the rest to demonstrate their zeal. Surprisingly enough, in view of the vastness of the undertaking, the slowness of travel and the inexperience of many participants, the valuation-books were in the hands of the Exchequer by the beginning of 1536.

The great collection of returns, known henceforth as the *Valor Ecclesiasticus* or the *King's Books*, is one of the few early national surveys which can be placed without a sense of incongruity alongside Domesday Book, and a student of Cromwellian administration cannot do better than peruse one of the six great folio volumes in which it was printed over a century ago by the Record Commissioners. Contemporary taxpayers regarded Cromwell as a hard-faced fiscal oppressor; as the satirist Brinklow remarked, the Latin Papa had been translated into the English Pay-Pay. The records of the Court of First-Fruits and Tenths show that between 1535 and 1538 these taxes yielded nearly £50,000 a year, a sum not much less than half the previous ordinary revenue of the Crown. Yet for all Cromwell's vigilance, the *Valor* undoubtedly represented an underestimate of clerical incomes in the year 1535. Again, while the great inflation soon increased the nominal values of most benefices, Cromwell's less enterprising successors remained content with the *Valor* assessments. By the latter half of the century the incidence of clerical taxation was thus already far lighter than Cromwell had planned; by the time tenths and first-fruits were assigned to the governors of Queen Anne's Bounty, the burden had become negligible.

Meanwhile, reports of sedition and unrest began to come in, and before the end of the second session of 1534, a Treason Act was passed, making it treasonable to will maliciously, or desire by words or writing, any bodily harm to the King, Queen, or heir-apparent; to deprive them of their dignity, title, name, or royal estates; to publish by writing or words that the King was a heretic, schismatic, tyrant, infidel or usurper; to detain any of the King's ships, ammunition or artillery. It is still commonly maintained that this Act for the first time in English history made high treason of seditious words, yet unquestionable evidence has been adduced to show that, even in the fifteenth century, words could constitute high treason in common law. Nevertheless, members of Parliament, in 1534 not yet scared by rebellion, felt the dangers which lurked within this statute. 'There was never more sticking at the passing of any Act than at the passing of the same,' wrote a contemporary, nor did the adverb 'maliciously', insisted upon by Parliament, go far to protect suspects. Yet the heavy-handedness of the measure lay less in the risk that totally blameless men would fall into traps, than in the fact that it rendered punishable by death any denial of the Royal Supremacy.

A subsequent Act of 1536, 'To extinguish the Authority of the Bishop of Rome', not only indulged in incivilities towards the Pope (who had in the previous year deprived Henry of his kingdom and absolved his subjects from their allegiance) but made it treason on the part of any clerical or lay official, should he refuse an oath renouncing all jurisdiction of the see of Rome and supporting the Royal Supremacy. In 1539 persons going overseas to avoid penalties arising from religious proclamations were also brought within the net of treason. Altogether, these treason laws and some at least of the proceedings taken under them may be regarded as the most genuinely oppressive aspect of the Cromwellian years. Our judgement upon them must, however, depend in part upon the reality of the seditious and rebellious opposition, upon the risks of civil war and invasion, by which England stood threatened. They reflect the fears of an almost unarmed monarchy, aware of the offence it had given to conservative opinion, and anxious to nip actual sedition in the bud. Given the Reformation-policy, the readiness of territorial magnates to play with treason, and the absence of a real police-machinery, this phase of plots and legislative counter-terror was almost bound to develop. In the words of a later Cromwell, 'the necessity was not feigned'. The revolution might be legalist, but it did not know how to remain liberal. For the linking of Catholic dissent with treason the neo-feudal opposition was as responsible as the government, yet the latter had plunged into fundamental changes involving both the consciences and the interests of its subjects, and throughout the rest of the century it found itself faced with a query all too familiar throughout the long aftermaths of historic revolutions. How does a nation stop the sinister pendulum-swing of revolution versus reaction? Tudor and Stuart Englishmen had no ready answer to this question. Violence bred counterviolence, and for a century and a half the ugly dialectic continued to disturb English society.

Cromwell himself was no vengeful persecutor; he has been greatly wronged by the seekers for personal scapegoats. At the same time, one cannot imagine him as ever taking a risk in the treatment of seditious activities: neither he nor any other sixteenth-century statesman would have conceived it possible to experiment with a liberal forbearance towards conspirators and rebels, proved or suspected. Could they return to answer modern criticism, they would no doubt argue that we misunderstand the alternatives which lay before them, and that they would have conferred small benefit upon the people committed to their charge had they allowed sedition to ripen into revolt and civil war. If Sir Thomas More's and Queen Mary's attitude towards heretics cannot be judged in the light of modern western standards, neither can the treason laws of Henry VIII and the penal code of Elizabeth. Both belong equally to the sixteenth century with its mental limitations and its harsh compulsions.

The end of the year 1534 saw the legal revolution in Church and State virtually completed. Whatever be thought of the ethical and theological issues involved, it must be acknowledged a technical triumph in the field of legislation. In our long history, no changes so momentous have ever been accomplished by statute within three years. Never before had a block of legislation so extensive and so closely co-ordinated passed through Parliament. Never had one step led so smoothly to another; never had lobbying been so effectively conducted; never had loopholes for opposition been closed with such remorseless efficiency. Once again the Crown was back under business management. After the gorgeous international advertising of Wolsey and the flounderings of lesser men, the ghosts of Empson and Dudley were enjoying a belated laugh. The new managing director had severed all connection with the big continental combine: he had even presumed to make a subsidiary firm of *ecclesia anglicana*. This severance and this merger had their convenience; indeed, they defined most prophetically some of the main features of English life in the centuries to come. Even so, the spirit of the nation was too ebullient, too emotional, too versatile to tolerate business-management unadorned. And quite apart from the claims of romance, the development of both Reformation and Counter Reformation were destined soon to produce some patterns uncongenial to tidy minds of a Cromwellian stamp.

Chapter Five

Cromwellian Ideas

THOSE who lack admiration for its conduct have naturally claimed that the Reformation Parliament was 'packed', and thus unrepresentative of the nation. It was no more packed, and no less so, than any other Tudor Parliament. Twentieth-century notions concerning fair representation and legitimate influence upon elections are irrelevant to Georgian Parliaments, let alone to those of Tudor times, when a large proportion of the Commons invariably consisted of royal servants and of men linked by special ties with the Crown or the chief ministers, when both ministers and independent magnates quite normally put pressure upon corporations to elect their adherents, when the sheriffs themselves frequently took a forceful hand in county elections. Readers of Sir John Neale's works on the Elizabethan Parliaments will be the first to see the absurdity of the old suggestions that Cromwell was offending against constitutional liberty in writing letters to request the election of certain individuals.

No error could be more fundamental than the notion that Cromwell was an antagonist of parliamentary institutions, the planner of a solitary despotism by the King. Such a plan, if it ever occurred to him, must have been dismissed as totally unrealistic. Under sixteenth-century circumstances, no English statesman worthy of employment would have pursued a scheme so bound to prove ineffective; no king with half the intelligence of Henry VIII would have embarked upon a course so hazardous to his survival. The personal powers of Henry VIII were extensive, yet they looked more extensive than they were. He ruled a tough and turbulent nation, which on grounds of self-interest had turned predominantly royalist, yet had never ceased to think for itself, to protect its legal and representative institutions, and even to be capable of rebellion. His task was to seize upon its prevalent mood and marshal it in the way it was going. The internal tension at this stage of our history did not arise between Crown and Parliament; it arose between the Crown in Parliament and the various *imperia in imperio*: neo-feudal family interests and affinities, jurisdictional liberties, and the Church seen as an independent source of jurisdiction. The monarchy was not conspicuously well equipped with its own instruments: its regular revenues were inadequate to meet any major crisis; it lacked a significant standing army or police-force; outside London it had little by way of a professional civil service. The North alone proved itself, under reactionary leadership, able to raise armed forces far more powerful than those at the ready disposal of the King. The textbook notion that Henry, by some condescending decision, 'took Parliament into partnership', means little to those who understand Tudor government. If he wanted to conduct a policy, the King had no alternative to such a partnership. Clad in the gilded trappings of arrogance and majestic affability, the Tudors had always to play to their public, both inside and outside Parliament; they had to play both to the stalls and to the gallery. When Henry said, 'We at no time stand so highly in our estate royal as in the time of Parliament', he was in part paying a compliment, yet he was also stating a cold fact.

So far as Thomas Cromwell is concerned, Dr. Elton has demonstrated the worthlessness of Reginald Pole's assertion that the minister wished to place the King above the law; he has also displayed the amplitude of the evidence which depicts Cromwell in his true character of common lawyer and parliamentarian. At every stage of his work, Cromwell set forth by precept and practice the legislative supremacy of the King in Parliament. He may be claimed as one of the greatest of our parliamentary statesmen, always provided it be remembered that the character and functions of Parliament in 1532 did not closely resemble those of 1832. It is the deceptive appearance of institutional continuity in English history which has most often lured our historians into confused thinking.

The notion of a despotic and Machiavellian Cromwell derives in very large part from the usual source, but in demonstrating the unreliable character of Pole's testimony, there is no need to vilify the witness himself, for his intentions were not dishonourable. His account of Cromwell's initial schemes was written in 1538, nine years after the chief events it purports to describe, but shortly after Cromwell had taken part in the prosecution of

75

Pole's relatives in England. In one passage he makes Cromwell conduct as early as 1529 a private interview with the King and with satanic subtlety tell him that kings are above the moral law. Henry is immediately convinced and promotes Cromwell (three years in advance of the actual date) to a place amongst his most intimate counsellors. The interview is not less fictitious than the alleged outcome, while Pole himself admits that he composed Cromwell's speech from sayings he had heard at various times. And while so near the topic, we may briefly review the common statement that Cromwell based his political theories and practices upon a study of Machiavelli. This also derives from Pole's account of 1538, from the passage where the writer describes the only personal interview he ever had with Cromwell. This interview had taken place ten years earlier, during Pole's last visit to England. The two were discussing the duties of counsellors, Pole having expressed the humanist viewpoint that a counsellor's first concern must be the honour and true interest of his Prince. This, alleges Pole, Cromwell ridiculed as an academic dictum of the schools. The counsellor must, in a real world, observe the way in which the Prince's will is inclined, even his unspoken desires. Armed with this knowledge, the counsellor must then find methods to ensure that the prince gets his way, while yet seeming to act with perfect virtue. Pole says he made no comment upon this impiety, but remembered it. Cromwell then belittled book-learning, yet remarked that if Pole wanted to learn from books, he himself had one by a recent author, most clever and subtle, who had not followed his own imaginations (like those of Plato's *Republic*, which after so many centuries still found no place among men), but the things which daily experience proved to be true. Cromwell then offered to lend Pole this book, since he saw 'what great danger I should run into, if I should engage in the conduct of affairs, especially those of princes, instructed only by the works of leisured though learned men, instead of learning from those who had added experience of realities to acuteness of mind'. But Pole never received the book, and he thought this was due to Cromwell's subsequent repentance of his self-revelation. That Cromwell had actually mentioned Machiavelli's *Prince* is not even suggested by Pole, who merely goes on to remark that he had later been informed by people who knew Cromwell's reading that the reference must have been to the *Prince*.

Some heavy doubts have been cast on several aspects of Pole's retrospective account of this interview. Concerning its broad tenor one need not feel totally sceptical, since it is easy to believe that Cromwell, in a characteristic mood of sardonic worldly wisdom, was guilty of baiting the complacent young humanist. Indeed, he may have said many of these things and in some sense have meant them, yet as an accurate and objective account of Cromwell's political sources and principles, the passage cannot claim acceptance. Pole did not leave the actual interview thinking of Cromwell as subject to diabolical inspiration; four years after he had left England, he was still writing to Cromwell in not merely courteous but amicable terms, and even as late as February 1537 his gentleman-usher Michael Throgmorton wrote to Richard Morison, then living in Cromwell's house, that Pole bore Cromwell a hearty affection. But then a dramatic change ensued, and for obvious reasons. By 1538 Pole was calling the minister the devil's emissary and the devil in human form; he doubts whether he should defile his pages with Cromwell's name, yet, as great bandits, murderers and parricides are named in history for everlasting ignominy, as devils are mentioned in the Scriptures, so he will name Cromwell. We also know that, when he himself finally came to read Machiavelli, Pole took the shocked view (which his English contemporaries did not share) and helped to get the book placed on the papal Index of Prohibited Books. What more natural than to deduce, amid the passions of 1538, that the English Satan must have been referring to his Italian counterpart?

The difficulties involved in Pole's story are obvious. The conversation occurred in 1528, but the *Prince* was not published until 1532. It says little or nothing about the duties of counsellors. Again, in or after 1537, Lord Morley presented Cromwell with a copy of the *Prince* and Machiavelli's *History of Florence*, recommending them as books which, even at this date, Cromwell did not know. True, Morley could well have been mistaken: it is even conceivable that Cromwell may have been sent a manuscript-copy of the *Prince* before its publication. Nevertheless such disharmonies do not enhance our confidence in Pole's story and deductions. The upshot remains that Cromwell cannot be proved either to have read, or not to have read, Machiavelli in 1528, though the odds seem against his having done so. Paul Van Dyke suggested that Cromwell might have been referring to

Castiglione's equally famous *Book of the Courtier*, published in 1528 and certainly possessed by him in 1530. This notion has possibly received too rough a treatment by recent writers, since Castiglione contains at least one passage very close to the discussion. 'The office of a good courtier', he says, 'is to know the prince's character and inclinations, and thus to enter tactfully into his favour according to need and opportunity.' Such a passage comes much nearer the mark than anything in Machiavelli, yet even so, we are entitled to remain unconvinced, since a recommendation to read the *Courtier* as a whole would seem a cumbrous method of administering the lesson in statesmanship intended by Cromwell.

These are amusing detective-problems, yet they remain largely irrelevant to a modern assessment of Cromwell's statecraft. It has already been observed that a man so well versed in affairs in Italy, in the Netherlands and at home had little to learn about 'Machiavellian' methods from reading the *Prince*. Machiavelli might more easily have imparted to Cromwell the converse side of his teaching: the somewhat naïve idealism which inspires him to free his country from anarchy and foreign domination. And the modern readers who are shocked at Cromwell's alleged preference for Machiavelli as against Plato's *Republic* will be those who have not yet read the latter!

One further charge against Cromwell concerns his possible sympathy with the autocratic principles of Roman law. This arises from a self-confessedly vague recollection by another bitter enemy, Bishop Gardiner, who makes Cromwell quote in debate before the King the old civil law maxim *quod principi placuit, legis habet vigorem*. Any minister of the time might in a suitable context have cited this tag. Maitland's contention that England stood in danger of a 'reception' of Roman Law during the period of Cromwell's ministry was satisfactorily demolished by Holdsworth, and no viable evidence suggests a policy of 'reception' on his part or on that of the Henrician government. And whereas such opponents as Gardiner and Tunstall were Roman lawyers by training, no important figure of the Cromwellian group boasted such a background. Its chief lay members, Lord Chancellor Audley and Sir Richard Riche, Solicitor-General and Chancellor of Augmentations, were also common lawyers through and through. Cromwell himself was a parliamentarian of long standing; when his fortunes lay on the knife edge, his solution had been to re-enter the Commons. Once in power, he used statute-law to solve all the problems of the realm and the volume of parliamentary legislation greatly expanded during his ministry.

In this context it may also be remarked that historians have persistently misunderstood the Proclamations Act of 1539. Amongst other things, it is true, this statute enacted that the King might, with the advice of his Council, set forth proclamations as binding upon the subject as an Act of Parliament, provided that they did no damage to estates, liberties or persons, and infringed no laws. No longer, however, can this be assigned a despotic connotation or be used to father autocratic designs upon Thomas Cromwell. No one disputes that proclamations were a common and utterly necessary instrument of day-to-day administration, both before and after the eight years during which the Act stood on the statute book. Cromwell seems, however, to have been one of those uncomfortable about their legal status and anxious to ground them upon the superior basis of statute-law. In July 1535, when Parliament was not sitting, it became necessary to prohibit the export of coin. Before issuing any proclamation, Cromwell consulted the judges, searched the statutes, and found an Act of Richard II upon which it could be based. Moreover, he somewhat nervously asked the law officers of the Crown what would have happened had no such relevant statute existed. He received the reply from the Lord Chief Justice that the King would nevertheless have been free to issue a proclamation 'of as good effect as any law made by Parliament'. Cromwell records that he was 'very glad to hear' this opinion, and the transaction displays him as one of those least attuned to the planning of a personal despotism by royal decree.

Forty years ago Mr. Adair displayed the chief purpose of the Proclamations Act as ultimately passed in 1539. This he found in its fourth clause, which lays down that conviction for breach of a proclamation must take place before a special court, consisting of the Privy Council and the chief judicial officers of the Crown, or at least half of them, while of eight named officials two must always be present. The clause thus set up a court similar to that of the Star Chamber as constituted by the famous act of 1487. If anything, it limited and institutionalized the royal prerogative. Owing, however, to the congestion of business confronting the Privy Council, this enforcement-plan failed to work, and after an attempt at amendment, the whole Act was repealed in

1547. Again, the repeal did not occur because Protector Somerset loved liberty more than Cromwell or Henry VIII; proclamations were in fact used more often and more arbitrarily by Somerset and his successors than by Henry VIII.

The state-papers and the preambles to the Cromwellian statutes also afford no ground for the belief that Cromwell was at any stage attempting to engineer a personal despotism. On the contrary, in the Dispensations Act there stands a very clear acknowledgement of the fact that King, Lords and Commons together exercised legislative supremacy. Cromwell stood in the tradition of Christopher St. German in upholding the omnicompetence of Parliament and statute-law, together with the all-embracing character of state-sovereignty which such law expressed. At his trial Sir Thomas More bravely denied this doctrine, yet the verdict of all subsequent English constitutional history has lain not with him, but with Cromwell. When Lord Burghley said there was nothing that an Act of Parliament could not do in England, he was not merely speaking in the Cromwellian tradition, but foreshadowing the orthodoxy which every modern student of our constitutional history imbibes from the classic pages of Dicey. When Cromwell persuaded the King to solve his problems by national legislation alone, the Papacy and the English clergy found themselves confronting an adversary far more formidable than a wilful autocrat : they stood face to face with what Cromwell called 'Your Royal Majesty and your Lords Spiritual and Temporal, and Commons, representing the whole state of your realm in this your most High Court of Parliament'. The facts corresponded quite closely with this official phraseology, and even the apparently foreign body in this organic structure—the Lords Spiritual—did not in fact behave as such. Almost every one of them swam with the tide, some eager, some uneasy, but only one accepting martyrdom and none embracing exile. With a certain ease and inevitability, Leviathan at last attained his full stature in England.

While the Reformation-statutes bore no resemblance to any previous programme of legislation, the campaign of propaganda which accompanied them was likewise a new and sensational development, for it represents the awakening of government to the political uses of the printing-press. Thanks chiefly to two American scholars, Dr. Baumer and Dr. Zeeveld, much is now known concerning the governmental writers and their books, yet these researches have not yet made the impact upon English histori ography and teaching which their merits demand. They have a special importance for those who seek to understand the genesis of Anglicanism. Copies are extant of nearly 50 books and editions published during Cromwell's ministry with the specific object of defending the new settlement, while in addition the press turned out a stream of proclamations, injunctions and other official material. At least 28 books were printed by the King's printer Berthelet; the rest, with very few exceptions, by London printers easily amenable to Crown influence. Conversely, the government denied the use of the English presses to its opponents. Directed in part by Cromwell himself, this propaganda swiftly responded to events. Within a few weeks of the outbreak of the Pilgrimage of Grace, at least four books were published to denounce the iniquities of rebellion. In the same year, Paul III summoned a General Council of the Church, and the royalists (some of whom had at earlier stages stressed the authority of such a Council) hastily produced tractates denying the Pope's right to make the summons. Likewise, on the overthrow of the Pole family, Richard Morison was immediately set to write a justification.

At the same time, Cromwell's publicists and the Henricians in general were by no means satisfied to write mere *livres de circonstance* or to produce utilitarian arguments for the Royal Supremacy. They wanted also to place the new policy upon a solid philosophical and scriptural basis; they wanted, moreover, to confer upon it the respectability of tradition and support it by reference to ancient and medieval theory. Like true men of the Renaissance, they grasped for the helping hands of past thinkers, yet they could not reasonably have expected these hands to be numerous: the ancient world showed no closely comparable patterns, while medieval thought in general enshrined the very traditions against which they were revolting. Yet at least one great rebel of earlier times seemed heaven-sent for their purpose, and a lapse of two centuries had conferred upon him, if not respectability, at least a patina of tradition. His thinking could moreover claim to be based upon that of the medieval demigod Aristotle, based as closely as any work of St. Thomas Aquinas or of the upholders of ecclesiastical prerogative. By any criteria Marsiglio of Padua must be accounted one of the portents of medieval scholarship. Theologian, medical doctor and for a time Rector of the University of Paris, he belongs to those Averroist groups of Paris and

Padua which included also the chief medieval ancestors of modern physical science. He completed his work *Defensor Pacis* in 1324 and, when its authorship became known, fled to the Emperor Louis of Bavaria, from whom he accepted high offices and whose excommunication at the hands of Pope John XXII he speedily shared. If Marsiglio's book sprang from a situation analogous to that of Henry VIII, its radicalism was so massive and profound as to make Henry's contemporaries, even Machiavelli himself, look timid. To Marsiglio the nation-state, based upon the legislative capacity of its people, is not only omnipotent but completely self-sufficent for all the purposes of man in this earthly portion of his life. The clergy should be as amenable as other men to the civil courts; they are not by right judges or owners, but merely physicians of the soul, concerned with the welfare of men in the next world. They have no jurisdiction in this one, unless it be specifically derived from the State; if, for example, heresy be punished on earth, it should be punished as a civil offence. Likewise the Church lacks real proprietary rights and merely uses what the State lends it : its property is a gift or subsidy made by the nation to support public worship. If it receives tithes, it does so by kind permission of the lay authority. Ecclesiastical office also lies within the gift of the civil power, which may not only compel ecclesiastics to perform such offices, but also depose them by civil action. The ecclesiastical hierarchy is of purely human institution, bishops and popes having no *spiritual* authority which a simple priest does not also possess. In merely ecclesiastical matters, a General Council, composed of priests and laymen, has the true title to supreme authority. No Pope can claim supremacy as the successor of Peter, who had no pre-eminence over the other apostles. There is, argues Marsiglio, no reliable evidence that Peter was in Rome, still less that he was a bishop; the ecclesiastical primacy of Rome springs from the position of the city as an imperial capital. Canon law itself holds no independent validity, and papal decretals have no legislative force, unless sanctioned by the national community. The Bible, in particular the New Testament, forms the only source of revelation and of divine law; hence only scriptural beliefs are necessary to salvation.

Such doctrines as these, in some places slightly expurgated, in others reinforced by arguments drawn from the *Dialogus inter militem et clericum* (a tract arising from the struggle of Philip le Bel with the Papacy, and englished in 1533) or from later thinkers like Wyclif and the champions of the Conciliar Movement, became formidable weapons in the hands of a government which found itself in conflict with a resurgent papalism. It cannot for a moment be questioned that Cromwell and his publicists were fully abreast of the Marsilian theories and thought themselves to be adapting these concepts of the Church-State relation to the needs of their day and their country. In 1535 Cromwell's henchman William Marshall published the first English translation of the *Defensor Pacis*, and Cromwell personally lent the money for this purpose. In that same year Thomas Starkey, his pamphleteer-in-chief, made liberal use of Marsiglio in *An Exhortation to the People, instructing them to Unity and Obedience*, a book which a recent writer has also called the earliest manifesto of the Anglican *via media*. Richard Sampson and Edward Fox had already in 1533-4 published books using Marsilio's doctrines to exclude the application of papal law to England. And it would be difficult to depict the Marsilian sovereign state more tersely than did Cromwell himself in that famous preamble to the Act of 1533 which restrained Englishmen from making appeals to the Roman courts. 'Whereas by divers sundry old authentic histories and chronicles, it is manifestly declared and expressed that this realm of England is an Empire . . . governed by one Supreme Head and King, having the dignity and royal estate of the imperial Crown of the same, unto whom a body politic, compact of all sorts and degrees of people, divided in terms and by names of spiritualty and temporalty, ben bounden and owen to bear, next to God, a natural and humble obedience'. Yet the Marsilian arguments by no means remained the preserve of Cromwell's circle, for no one used them to more devastating effect than did Stephen Gardiner in his *De Vera Obedientia*.

Of the actual Cromwellian group, perhaps the most interesting was Thomas Starkey, an able humanist and former Fellow of Magdalen, who had spent some congenial years in the household of Reginald Pole at Venice and Padua. At the end of 1534 he returned to serve as chaplain to Pole's mother the Countess of Salisbury, but having approached Cromwell for patronage, soon found himself a royal chaplain. Shortly afterwards Starkey sent Cromwell an essay on the Aristotelian concept of Man and the State, recalling in the preface that it had been written at his patron's specific request. 'It pleased you to demand of me, what thing it is after the sentence of Aristotle and the Peripatetics, that commonly among them is called Policy.' This essay contained the basis of Starkey's *Dialogue between Pole and Lupset*, the book for which Starkey is now best known, but which was not destined to publication until 1871. Even if the author had not made Pole his chief interlocutor, its subject-matter would have made it unpublishable under Henry VIII. Starkey was a forerunner of the liberal 'Commonwealth Party' and entertained trenchant views concerning English social and economic evils. In proposing remedies, the *Dialogue* even went so far as to suggest making the monarchy elective on the King's death. Cromwell can scarcely have encouraged his *protégé* in such daring speculations, yet he conducted further discussions with Starkey, who soon sent him a second essay forming the core of his *Exhortation to the People*. Clear evidence shows that he redrafted the original version of this work in accordance with criticisms expressed by Cromwell and others.

In thinking of Thomas Starkey, one should certainly avoid the impression of a hack-writer paid to bolster authoritarian government and Protestantism, for anyone answering less to this formula could not be imagined. Starkey was a fundamental thinker endeavouring to conduct the controversy upon the highest philosophical level; he was not only the champion of an enlightened social policy, but a would-be reconciler of the warring parties. If anything, he showed more tenderness towards the Catholics than to the Protestants. Henry and Cromwell had placed high hopes in his ability to win over the troublesome Pole, and on the latter's violent defiance in 1536, Starkey fell into disfavour and retired to his benefice in Sussex. Again active in official business the following year, he preached to the King shortly before his early death in August 1538.

A more prolific and successful member of the group was Richard Morison, presumably known to Cromwell since his early days in Wolsey's household. Having gone to Italy to study Greek, he fell into poverty, pawned his books to the Jews and ended as a recipient of Pole's bounty, and wearing a pair of breeches lent by one of Pole's gentlemen. By 1535 he was busily ingratiating himself with Cromwell, who in the following year paid his passage home with the express purpose of utilizing his literary talents. Morison had already written his *Apomaxis*, a counterblast to the attack of the German Catholic controversialist Cochlaeus upon the divorce and the Royal Supremacy, a book which finally appeared in 1537 with a fulsome dedication to Cromwell. Morison's connection with Pole had been much more superficial than that of his friend Starkey, and on Pole's defiance he unhesitatingly denounced his former benefactor as 'an evil-willed man'. To Cromwell he wrote, 'I am a graft of your Lordship's own setting and will stand in no other's ground. Other men have but tickled the Pope. I have so pricked him that men shall say I know how to anger popes. Would it were the answer to Mr. Traitor Pole's book.' It is hard to assess the sincerity of this amusing and clever humanist. He possibly belongs to that not inconsiderable category of intellectuals whose enthusiasm for a cause finds powerful stimulous from a good salary. Nevertheless, it is easy to underestimate the influence of patriotism on such men. Morison seems thoroughly convinced of his own sincerity and, to do him justice, he continued loudly to proclaim his personal loyalty to Cromwell as late as May 1540, when more prudent friends were silent in the face of impending catastrophe. His moment of glory had come during the crisis of 1536-7, when, closely directed by the King and Cromwell, he thundered most loudly of all the pamphleteers upon the theme of loyalty. On this theme Morison also shows himself more than a writer of *livres de circonstance*, for like Starkey he evinces an excellent grasp of the social and economic causes of popular discontent. He was also probably the first Englishman to acquire a close and perceptive knowledge of Machiavelli.

A third member of the circle was the publisher and translator William Marshall, a violent anti-papalist known to have produced books for Cromwell from April 1534. The next year he borrowed the £20 from his patron in order to produce his translation of Marsiglio. The total cost of this edition amounted to £34, and poor sales resulted in an action for debt brought against Marshall and his brother by John Gostwick, Treasurer of First-Fruits. Marshall then appealed to Cromwell to obtain a stay of this action and seemingly remained in business, since he published an abridgement of *Münster's Chronicle* as late as 1542. Marshall has also been suggested as the possible author of a prophetic scheme for a Poor Law made in 1535 at Cromwell's request. More important to the minister's designs was Richard Taverner, a former member of the Protestant cell at Cardinal

College, who returned destitute from a period of study abroad and solicited help from Cromwell. In 1532 the latter persuaded the Duke of Norfolk to give him a small pension, but Taverner is called 'Cromwell's client' in 1533, and three years later he obtained his patron's nomination as Clerk of the Privy Seal. He was meanwhile writing vigorously to further the cause of the Reformation. A full-blooded Protestant, he translated Melanchthon and Sarcerius, and he lived not only to see his books burned at Paul's Cross in 1546, but also to sample peace and prosperity under Elizabeth. His translation of the Bible will shortly meet our attentions. Concerning the precise relations of various other publicists with Cromwell, we should gladly learn more: one of these was Thomas Gibson, the medical doctor who turned to printing and may have been the man warmly recommended in 1537 by Latimer to Cromwell as a cheap and conscientious publisher able to do good service in the cause. Gibson's press appears to have been almost entirely devoted to his own works, both medical and, in the cases of at least three books, anti-papalist in character. Clement Armstrong, an elderly London businessman of obvious sincerity but mediocre literary gifts, took to writing in the last years of his life (1533–6), and sent Cromwell two economic treatises, which have become well known in recent years. But even Armstrong's zeal was probably based on religious enthusiasm, for also among Cromwell's papers are his 'sermons and declarations against popish ceremonies'.

The Cromwellian writers were thus a heterogeneous body, and their leading ideas cannot easily be crystallized in a few sentences. On the doctrinal side, as Dr. Zeeveld has shown, their most fruitful concept was that of *adiaphora*, the category of 'things indifferent' and unnecessary to salvation: for example, fish-eating on Friday, pilgrimage, holy days, prayers to saints and even papal authority, as not expressly commanded in the Scriptures. Like Frith before him, Starkey derived this concept from Melanchthon and gave it classic expression in the *Exhortation*. Those who squabble over *adiaphora*, he urges, are blind children of darkness: keep to the middle path, avoiding irrational superstition on the one hand and arrogant personal opinion on the other. When readers asked whence a ruling between things necessary and things indifferent should come, Starkey told them in effect to leave the problem to Parliament. Cromwell lent his personal adherence to this viewpoint; one imagines it must have attracted him for a variety of reasons; his own cool temperament, his distrust of **dog**-matic priests, his ambitions to confer peace on the realm and to achieve an understanding with the Lutheran princes. Again, he can hardly have been blind to the likelihood that he and his group would more easily achieve survival in a broad-minded and tolerant climate. Yet the mingled religious and political appeal of adiaphorism was far from being limited to its originators. It appears not only in Starkey, in Morison, in Taverner, in the Ten Articles of 1536, but also in the Thirty Nine Articles (Nos. XX, XXXIV) and in Jewel, Hooker, Whitgift and other Elizabethans. It became one of the pillars of the Anglican *via media* and may reasonably be taken as an early milestone along the thorny path towards religious toleration.

All the Henrician propagandists became in some measure Marsilians, and like their inspirer sought not merely to free the national state from papal jurisdiction, but also to limit the powers of the clergy to genuinely spiritual spheres. Approaching this latter problem with the terminology of the canon law, they transferred *jurisdictio fori* to the King in Council or the King in Parliament. This term included all the judicial, coercive and legislative functions of the Church, even the power to define doctrine. To the clergy they left *potestas ordinis*, what St. German called 'mere spiritual things': the power to consecrate and to administer the sacraments. Like the rest of the Henricians, Cromwell's group supported the transfer of powers, while specifically rejecting any proposal to ascribe *potestas ordinis* to the King. Neither the latter nor his minister desired to place such spiritual functions in the hands of any layman. Chapuys, it is true, reports that Cromwell summoned certain bishops before the Council to ask them whether the King could not make and unmake bishops, but there is not the slightest reason to suppose that here *faire et refaire* relates to consecration. So long as the King could nominate the bishops, he was not interested in consecrating them; so long as he could say how many sacraments were necessary to salvation, he had no ambition to administer them in person. Whatever the impossibility of secular despotism, once the Royal Supremacy over the English Church came to be discussed, there were inevitably those who tended to envisage it as inherent in the person of the King rather than as a function of the King in Council or in Parliament. The most alarming phraseology of this type is probably to be found in Tyndale, or, at the other extreme, in Gardiner. So far as I have observed, the outlook of the Cromwellians and of St. German is, like that of their leader, more institutional and parliamentarian. In relation to the Church as to the State, they cannot be depicted as propagandists of autocracy. They tend to retain the old, limiting concept of a Natural Law; they are not adulators of Roman law; they proclaim the duties of the monarch as loudly as his privileges, and they reiterate the solemnity of his responsibility before God.

With such canonist concepts as *jurisdictio fori* and *potestas ordinis*, writers like Starkey and Morison are not primarily concerned: these could be left to the technical experts like Gardiner and Fox, who wrote in Latin for the learned of Europe. The Cromwellians were humanists with the background of poor scholars rather than that of great officials; they were charged by their employer to write in English and aim their arguments at the reading-public and even at the masses of the English nation. Their social outlook squares with this approach; also with the bourgeois forces which had come to play an increasing part in English public life under Wolsey and, still more pointedly, under Cromwell. While these publicists denounce the sin of rebellion and urge acceptance of the existing constitutional structure, it must be remembered that in 1536 rebellion was not levelling but aristocratic in character.

Wherever one looks, the emphases of Cromwell and his associates lie upon the opening of careers to men of talent, whatever their birth. Many needy scholars found in Cromwell a benefactor, 'especially', as one put it, 'of poor men, whom you are always glad to help'. Morison appeals to Cromwell by saying that nobility and learning do not go together; later on he staunchly asserts (with Dante!) that ability and character are the true aristocracy. Starkey insists that God does not respect birth; both of them, like Cromwell himself, see the social and the religious problems of their age as demanding above all a scheme of popular education. Similarly Cranmer, another man of the people, opposed in noble words a plan to restrict the King's School, Canterbury, to the sons of gentlemen, while Cromwell, in his Injunctions of 1536, ordered rich clergy to maintain poor scholars at the universities. When the Duke of Norfolk suggested that only noblemen could keep order in the Marches, Cromwell and Cranmer headed the group of councillors who put him in his place: 'If it shall please his Majesty to appoint the meanest man . . . to rule and govern in that place, is not his Grace's authority sufficient to cause all men to serve his Grace under him without respect of the very estate of the personage?' There is obviously nothing surprising in these relatively democratic emphases when *parvenus* were themselves in power, but today, when doctrinaires so often over-stress the contrary aspects of the Reformation, it is important to realize the early strength of this fund of social liberalism on the Protestant side. Unfortunately, its adherents could convert neither Henry nor Norfolk. As for Cromwell, he laid the founda-tions of a social policy in terms of order, legality and adminis-trative institutions, but had not the time, even if he be credited with the will, to move far along the road desired by Starkey and later by the Commonwealth Party. By the reign of Edward VI, this party no longer stood unchallenged in the leadership of English Protestantism, for the more self-interested nobility and gentry had by then cashed in upon the cause and deprived it of any special claims to social idealism. The humanist clerics and bourgeois intellectuals had the best ideas, but their political influence remained as insecure and as vulnerable as that of their patron, Thomas Cromwell.

Chapter Six

Cromwell's Opponents

THE ideals and achievements of the Cromwellian policy cannot be appreciated without some understanding of the complex forces against which the minister was striving. These forces ranged from the highest idealism to the lowest selfishness and irrationalism; so heterogeneous a collection of saints, heroes, politicians, dupes and fools cannot be dismissed with a few labels and generalizations. The conservative opponents of Cromwell, so often lumped together by their admirers and their critics, differed widely on all the significant criteria: the genuineness of their religious motives; their understanding of the causes involved; their loyalties to the Tudor State; their attitudes to the menace of neo-feudalism; their views of the divorce, the Papacy, the plan to dethrone Henry VIII, the prospect of a Spanish-Imperial invasion. At no point can the religious or ecclesiastical history of the Reformation be neatly abstracted from this surrounding *mêlée* of personal, political and economic motives. During Cromwell's ministry there were many opposition-movements, but no co-ordinated opposition-party with a colourable claim to replace the King or even to choose his ministers. A common hatred of the upstart Cromwell must not be confused with a common policy, or even with a common ideal.

Apart from the cases of More and Fisher, the most purely and sincerely religious opposition arose from certain members of the two liveliest religious bodies, the Franciscan friars of the strict Observance and the monks of the Carthusian order. The Observants of Greenwich, founded by the King's father, had been his closest monastic associates, and both his daughters had been baptized in their church. In May 1534 William Peto, one of their most eminent preachers, compared Henry with Ahab, and this to his face. When one of the royal chaplains attempted a counter-sermon, he was attacked from the eminence of the roodloft by Warden Elstow, who called him one of the four hundred prophets into whom the spirit of lying was entered, and who sought to establish the succession by adultery. This again happened in the King's presence and, not very surprisingly, both friars found themselves before the Privy Council. Here they were rebuked by the lords, while, according to Stow, the Earl of Essex told them they deserved to be put in a sack and cast into the Thames. The Earl's name happened incidentally to be Henry Bourchier, not Thomas Cromwell, as Canon Dixon supposed. Elstow, more than equal to the occasion, replied that he should say these things to rich and dainty folk, who had their chief hope in this world; as for the friars, they 'knew the way to heaven to be as ready by water as by land'. At this early stage, the law of verbal treasons had not yet been framed, and the punishment of the Observants proceeded along cumbrous lines. In June the whole order was suppressed, their six houses handed over to the Augustinians, their more obstinate members sent to the Tower, and the rest enclosed in the houses of the unreformed Greyfriars. Some died in prison and many suffered banishment. Of the latter a number, including Peto and Elstow, returned to England under Queen Mary; the superb intrepidity of the former even had its reward in this world, for he survived to become a cardinal, having been suggested for the office of Legate to England.

Though the Carthusian order was more deeply divided, the majority of its members who accepted the Royal Supremacy did so under pressure and with deep misgivings. In April 1535 John Houghton, prior of their London house, together with Robert Lawrence, prior of Beauvale and Augustine Webster, prior of Axholme, denied in the presence of Cromwell that the King as a layman could be Head of the Church. With them stood Dr. Reynolds, a learned Bridgettine of Sion, and John Haile, vicar of Isleworth, who was under the influence of Sion, in its turn a house closely related to those of the Carthusian order. Subsequently tried and condemned, all five followed each other to the gibbet with heroic constancy in May 1535; a few weeks later, three other London Carthusians were similarly condemned and several others distributed to the 'safe' houses of their order. Ten went to Newgate and all died of prison-fever, save one who suffered execution. Like Fisher and More, these Carthusians stand among the most genuine martyrs for Catholicism, 'not less beautiful', wrote Froude with a flash of generosity, 'not less deserving the everlasting remembrance of mankind, than those three hundred who in the summer morning sat combing their golden hair in the passes of Thermopylae'. The details have often been recounted with justifiable horror, but it is a horror which should be directed against the insensitivity of the age rather than against individuals or parties. Protestants, Catholics, politicians and common men were equally hardened to these spectacles and equally guilty of inflicting them. It is hard to say which was the more atrocious: a butchery for treason, a burning for heresy, or the slower torments of Tudor dungeon-life. All were accepted with equanimity by an age inured both to physical pain and to witnessing its infliction upon others. Equally unattractive is the sentiment expressed by Cromwell's assistant Bedyll, when he reported that the Carthusians in Newgate 'be almost despatched by the hand of God'. This curious attitude was also shared by mid-Tudor men of all parties; it was Bishop Gardiner who wrote that by Queen Katherine's death 'God had given sentence' in the divorce-suit.

A very different ecclesiastical oppositionist was Reginald Pole, even more Italianate than Cromwell, living in comfortable exile on the Continent while helping to weave those webs of English conspiracy which strangled so many of his friends and relatives. His mother, Margaret Countess of Salisbury, was a niece of Edward IV and sister of that Earl of Warwick whom Henry VII had executed in 1499, the year before the birth of Reginald. Though the latter and his elder brothers, Lord Montague and Sir Geoffrey Pole, were thus scions of the White Rose, Henry VIII held him in affectionate esteem and paid for his education with the Carthusians of Sheen and at Magdalen College, Oxford. From 1521 to 1526 Reginald Pole continued to cultivate his mind amongst the eminent scholars of Padua; already he was cherished by Bembo and Erasmus alike. A kindly master and patron of scholars, he attracted especial attention by a strict morality and a precise religious observance then unusual in men of his station. Returning to England, he remained a *protégé* of the admiring King, who in 1527 made him Dean of Exeter. And no one grumbled when Pole continued his delightful and scholarly life in the charming house which Colet had built at Sheen. During this period, which saw his famous interview with Cromwell, he disapproved the divorce-plans, honourably refused offers of the sees of York and of Winchester, and tried mildly to dissuade the King without provoking his wrath. In 1530 he took part, however reluctantly, in advancing Henry's cause in the European universities. Two years later he obtained permission to leave England for purposes of study, and spent some months pursuing theology at Avignon. As the winds of France did not suit his health and he longed for his second country, he soon returned to Padua, to his humanist friends Bembo and Flaminio.

He had not, however, slipped from the memory of the King and Cromwell, who pressed him through his former chaplain Thomas Starkey to acknowledge the royal claims. In 1536, however, he ceased to temporize, and in his book *De Unitate Ecclesiae* denounced Henry with a savagery which perhaps only cultivated men in their rare moments of resolution can attain. There lingers about the book and about Pole's mind a strange unreality, enhanced by an academic rhetoric conspicuously febrile even by the standards of the High Renaissance. We have already noted his inconsistencies in regard to Cromwell, but these are minor examples of their type. In his book he at once professes his grieved affection for Henry and accuses him of wholesale murder, sacrilege, robbery, waste, perjury, adultery and lust. Henry is worse than the Tunisian pirates, the Grand Turk, Nero and Domitian; he is worthy to have upon his tomb that epitaph of Sardanapalus, which Aristotle said was fitter for a bull than for a man. Indeed, the King was scarcely worthy of a tomb, but rather, in Isaiah's words, to be cast out from his sepulchre as a useless trunk, and as a putrid corpse to have no fellowship with his forefathers. All this Pole sincerely uttered long before he had any personal reasons for hating the King or the minister, under the absurd impression that it might bring Henry back into the Roman allegiance. More strangely still, he wrote on 16 February 1537, to the Privy Council: 'You say the Pope is the King's enemy, to which I reply thus: I dare to affirm of this Pope, whose acts I see, whose talk I often hear, that I have never heard of a single act or word of his, either concerning the King or concerning those who are in his kingdom, which did not show the affection of a father, and that indeed the most indulgent father towards his son, or the affection of a most loving pastor towards his flock'. This amazing statement he wrote on the eve of his departure to aid the northern insurrection in England, a mission which the Pope himself explained to the Spanish ambassador, and which Pole's own letters show him fully to have understood. Moreover, he was later to write to Edward VI denying that he had in 1539 attempted to induce other kings to take up arms against Henry, and asserting that he had merely intended to persuade the Emperor and the King of France to use the reasoning of love and friendship with Henry. This statement has again been directly disproved by reference to Pole's own writings. We may ironically imagine the terms which certain of Pole's admirers would apply to Henricians or Protestants guilty of such inconsistencies, yet even so, we should be unjust to accuse him of deliberate untruth. He had a bad memory, a retiring and fundamentally unambitious man's distaste for an enforced political role, together, perhaps, with a self-hypnosis accomplished by the instrument of his own rhetoric. Yet this is the writer upon whose testimony, assisted by that of Chapuys, the accepted picture of Thomas Cromwell is to a quite surprising degree based.

Chapuys told the Emperor that if Pole went home, the King would make him a cardinal by the same method as he had made one of Bishop Fisher. Pope Paul III, ignoring this last unfortunate precedent, then overcame Pole's objections and made him both cardinal and Legate to England. By this time, February 1537, the Pilgrimage of Grace had already collapsed. Lack of speed, resolution and nerve had prevented Pole and his backers from leaving English history the romantic spectacle of a White Rose Cardinal Legate riding at the head of an embattled host of north country feudalists. The importance of his defiance, however little personal heroism it involved, should not be underestimated. In view of the drastic nature of the revolution, it is a surprising fact that Pole was the only eminent Englishman, clerical or lay, who took the trouble to escape abroad and raise the standard against the King. Through his known connections with the opposition nobility in England, he became a focus of papal and Spanish enmity towards the kingdom. Like the Elizabethan *émigrés*, he misjudged the situation at home, misled foreigners with his illusory authority, imperilled the lives of his fellow-believers in England, ruined his own family and terminated what little hope existed that the governmental attitude might be liberalized. Unsatisfied with casting him for this overdramatic role, destiny had also in store for him a brief hour of glory as the spiritual husband of Mary Tudor, this too in an uncongenial world of flames and tears.

So far as concerns effective opposition to Cromwellian policy, the career of Pole has less significance than the Pilgrimage of Grace, the true crisis of the dynasty. In this great northern rising, the opposition did more than resort to arms; it showed itself able, at least in the short run, to muster a force far superior to that at the King's disposal. But for the confused minds of the rebel leaders, the fundamental class-divisions of the movement and the successful duplicity of the professional politicians, the kingdom would at this stage have fallen into bloodshed, perhaps into prolonged anarchy. The detailed events of the Pilgrimage have often been told, and they cannot become our present concern. It engulfed Lincolnshire early in October 1536, but there it died out within the month. Meanwhile, almost the whole of the northern counties had risen under the lawyer Robert Aske, had occupied York and received the surrender of Pontefract Castle, the key to the North: this at the hands of its keeper Lord Darcy, who joined the leaders. After prolonged negotiations with the Duke of Norfolk at Doncaster, the rebels dispersed early in December upon promises of reform and the offer of a free pardon. In January 1537 new risings in Cumberland and in Yorkshire— the latter led by Cromwell's former associate Sir Francis Bigod— gave Henry the excuse he had been awaiting and resulted in a total of some 200 executions, including those of Darcy, Aske and several other leaders of the main revolt. When causes are sought, the extremely voluminous records give rise to severe problems. In particular, the manifestoes of the educated leaders have been elaborately analysed, under the impression that here if anywhere the true causes of the trouble would become apparent. Yet these documents hardly begin to explain why the masses had become inflammable. As so often with mass-revolts, the major task of interpretation is to discover how far the material discontents of the people were guided into political and religious channels by doctrinaire leaders.

In the case of the Pilgrimage, economic troubles play an enormous rôle both inside and outside the 'official' lists of grievances. So far as concerns Cumberland and Westmorland, no one has ever denied that the rising was almost solely economic and social in its motives and manifestations: it was directed from first to last against enclosures and against the increased fines imposed by lords upon tenants entering upon their lands. Elsewhere in the North the same factors achieved much prominence on the eve of the Pilgrimage. In Craven in June 1535 and at York in May 1536 enclosure-riots had caused severe apprehension. Much evidence also attests the bad crops and high grain-prices current in the North in 1534-6. At York and Beverley the ancient group-conflicts between the close oligarchies of the councils and the unprivileged townsmen had again become rampant, while the clothiers of the West Riding joined the Pilgrimage because Parliament had just laid fierce penalties upon their fraudulent practices. The North suffered from lack of coin; its towns were few and small, its middle-classes relatively unimportant, its potential resources undeveloped. The gentry, though divided by faction, had their own range of grievances. The Statute of Uses prevented their settling portions upon younger sons and crippled their power to borrow by making mortgages illegal. They disliked the treason laws and resented the under-representation of the North in Parliament. Desiring a scapegoat for every grievance, all social classes simplified the issue by blaming Cromwell; they believed in that comic caricature : bluff, good-hearted King Hal, misled by a lowborn, heretical minister.

To do them justice, Cromwell had not handled northern opinion with outstanding tact. While he had recently put the Grand Jury of Yorkshire into the Star Chamber for acquitting an alleged murderer, he had also protected a servant of his nephew from the consequences of slaying a servant of Sir Ralph Eure. But in that world of seething, unpredictable faction, the Eures became the chief champions of the Crown in East Yorkshire, while Cromwell's own friend, the puritan Sir Francis Bigod, was the chief rival of the Eures, and turned rebel. The affair of the jury certainly seems to have been by far the chief reason for Cromwell's extreme local unpopularity. Robert Aske wrote that 'the Lord Cromwell . . . for the extreme assessment of their fines, was and yet is, in such horror and hatred with the people of those parts, that in manner they would eat him, and esteem their griefs only to arise by him and his counsel.' He had also incurred hatred for the disinheritance of Sir Thomas Percy, whose brother Northumberland, the ailing and wretched ex-lover of Anne Boleyn, had just made the King his heir. The Pilgrimage was certainly a Percy rising, despite the non-participation of the Earl. Most of its leaders were Percy-adherents and the name of

Percy still meant far more than that of Tudor throughout most of the region. Meanwhile, the interest of the House of York had become negligible, and even if Reginald Pole had succeeded in joining the rebellion, his Yorkist descent would probably have engaged no extra support. In general the North formed a strange mixture of class-tensions and feudal habits of mind. It had a pathetic belief in 'natural' leaders, and hated Cromwell, not merely for his actions and alleged actions, but for his lowly origins. The populace often forced highly unwilling gentry to swear fealty to the Pilgrimage and then submitted to their leadership. On the other hand, the government defeated the revolt largely by playing upon the divergent interests of the classes.

The nature of the problem which faced Cromwell in this antiquated but militarily vigorous society may best be exemplified in the case of Lord Darcy, that *beau ideal* of the romantic historians, and his noble associates. Long before the rising, Darcy had become the willing agent of Chapuys, the arch-enemy who stood at the centre of a network of oppositionist noblemen and supposed that revolt only needed to be set in motion in order to overthrow the dynasty. The two heroes of the Pilgrimage most *persona grata* at the Imperial embassy were Lords Darcy and Hussey. The latter, to whom Henry had entrusted the guardianship of the Princess Mary, sought out Chapuys to announce the plans for a northern rising and to appeal for the help of the Emperor. At the New Year of 1534 Darcy sent Chapuys a medal with the arms of Pole quartered with the leopards and lilies of England; well before the end of the year he was urging Charles V to an invasion of England and giving innumerable other evidences of treason. He announced to Chapuys that he would countenance Henry's offences no longer, but would go to the North, where every parish priest would preach against the heretic King and 1,600 lords and gentlemen would rally to the crucifix and the Imperial standard. The ambassador, duly gratified, put him in touch with the Earl of Northumberland and with his own brother-in-law Lord Sandys, governor of Guisnes and considered the first soldier in England. Darcy himself was not only a soldier of experience, but stood among the major northern magnates, for he boasted that he could raise 8,000 men amongst his tenants and friends. Besides Hussey and himself, an even greater figure of northern feudalism became embroiled in these schemes at an early date. Sir Thomas Dacre, Lord Dacre of the

North and Warden of the Western Marches, had already been intriguing with the Scots. Despite the efforts of Henry and Cromwell, his peers had acquitted him of the charge, and he had returned to the North bent on revenge. All these activities would have been difficult to justify by the feudal standards of an earlier age, but Darcy had become a veritable pillar of the Tudor state. Since 1498 he had held innumerable important northern offices; he was now the leading member of the King's Council in the North and constable of the key-fortress of Pontefract.

Whatever his former actions, they were eclipsed by his conduct during the rising itself. As chief counsellor north of Trent, he was writing to the King throughout the earliest days assuring him of his great efforts to suppress the trouble. Then at the appropriate moment Darcy joined its leadership and handed over Pontefract. If the enthusiasm of his admirers survives a close study of the facts, they will find themselves exalting some strange values. Can a man so deliberately play a double game of loyalty and treason and yet be credited with the 'knightly sense of honour' attributed to Lord Darcy? Can solemn oaths to the Crown and the acceptance of its high offices be morally reconciled with this record? How could a militarily weak government meet this duplicity save with counter-duplicity? Can one feel surprise that Henry became ever more suspicious and revengeful against noble suspects, when such great servants of the State thought themselves free at any moment to call in foreign invaders, surrender his fortresses, and mobilize with his musterrolls the most martial part of the realm to overthrow his government? That Darcy had fine courage, generous instincts and deep piety, that he never thought his own honour impugned; those very facts illustrate all the more vividly the maladies afflicting the still violent, individualist and half-feudal society which Thomas Cromwell was attempting to administer and to transform.

The case of that other leader of the Pilgrimage, Robert Aske, cannot be discussed in the same terms. Little is known about the career and outlook of this able lawyer, beyond what may be gathered from the long and attractive confession he wrote at the King's request after the rising. Unlike Darcy, he was bound by no extraordinary obligations to the King; so far as we know, he had not engaged in treasonable plotting with foreign powers before the Pilgrimage; certainly he was a sincere idealist, whose personal magnetism brought him in a curiously spontaneous fashion to the leadership of the movement. Re-reading the records, the present writer has been impressed by the degree to which the element of religious enthusiasm seems to centre around the personality of Aske and around some few of his clerical supporters. For a brief space, these men succeeded in welding together the inchoate mass of secular fears and grievances into a crusade with a genuine if short-lived and fragile bond of religious emotion.

The many writers who have analysed the causes of the Pilgrimage of Grace naturally have a category called 'religious grievances', yet this seems to me the most complex category of all. Much of it can only be called religious in the loose sense that it shows connection with the ecclesiastical policy of the Crown. Heresy was not the primary issue. The petition of the Pilgrims that the Lutheran and Anabaptist heresies should be destroyed can have given no offence to the King, who was assiduously avoiding entanglement with the Confession of Augsburg and who was ere long to extend his persecution of the new religions. Whatever the Pilgrimage may have been, it was not a struggle between Catholics and Protestants. At this supreme crisis of his reign, Henry owed the preservation of his throne to two great magnates, the Duke of Norfolk and the Earl of Shrewsbury, who both detested and, wherever possible, persecuted the Reformers. The plea made at Pontefract that the Supremacy 'touching the cure of souls' should be reserved to the see of Rome was certainly the view of Aske and of certain other petitioners. At one point of his confession, Aske, himself a man of exceptionally strong religious views, says that 'every man grudged' against the Statute of Supremacy, because it would cause England to be divided from the Universal Church. The rest of the voluminous evidence shows that this statement must be viewed with caution. The Lincolnshire commons actually professed themselves ready to accept the Royal Supremacy. Darcy himself did not consider the exclusion of the Pope to be against the Faith, though he and Constable agreed to Aske's request to include the papal claim amongst the official articles. In an extant memorandum, which may be Aske's own, the compromise-suggestion is made that, out of reverence for tradition, the Roman spiritual headship should be acknowledged, but that in effect it should be exercised through the two English archbishops, 'so that the said Bishop of Rome shall have no further meddling'. In the end, the lay leaders left the problem of the Supremacy to be discussed by a group of divines, who, though under strong personal pressure from Aske to think along papalist lines, were characteristically divided on the whole issue, some of them having practical experience of the difficulties and disadvantages of papal jurisdiction in England. Altogether, it would be more than imaginative to depict the Pilgrimage of Grace as a vehemently papalist crusade.

The dissolution of the monasteries, usually regarded on the strength of a phrase in Aske's narrative as the 'chief cause' of the Pilgrimage, cannot without even more absurd simplification he dismissed as a religious grievance. Aske gives, it is true, his own defence of the monasteries; he argues a reasonable, if one-sided and lawyerly case, drawing his examples from the best type of religious house. Yet he also makes it clear that this personal view of the monasteries and their dissolution was not that of the mass of the pilgrims. Little attention has been paid to that other portion of his account which relates how, in an interview at Pontefract, he had described to the lords and gentry the grievances of the common people. The latter, he had urged, feared that rents, first-fruits and tenths would now be drained out of the north parts. 'By occasion whereof, within short space of years, there should be no money nor treasure in those parts, neither the tenant to have to pay his rents to the lord, nor the lord to have money to do the King service withall, for so much as in those parts was neither the presence of his Grace, execution of his laws, nor yet but little recourse of merchandise, so that of necessity the said country should either "patysh" [i.e. make a treaty] with the Scots, or for very poverty be enforced to make commotion and rebellion.' In other words, we have the positive statement of the idealist Aske that, to the common man, the dissolution was an economic grievance. Rather should one say a potential economic grievance, for in September 1536 the dissolution of the smaller monasteries was barely completed, and the greater ones stood untouched. For many reasons, these evil results did not fully materialize, and at least one of the reasons sprang from a deliberate act of government: the establishment of the King's Council in the North, which improved public order, promoted trade and defended tenant-right. The assumption by the rebels that the Cromwellian government had only predatory plans for the North turned out to be one of their deepest misconceptions.

Towards the monasteries the behaviour of the rebels varied very widely; in a few cases they reinstated the monks, in several others they behaved with considerable hostility towards them. The attitude of the monks themselves proved consistent: they took almost no part in the Pilgrimage and, as leading property-owners, lacked enthusiasm for the spectacle of mobs of armed peasants at their gates. Anything less like a crusade united by a disinterested ardour to re-establish monasticism would be impossible to conceive.

While the situation with respect to the monasteries thus proved highly complex, the rising as a whole had some strongly irrational elements, which make delightful reading, but discourage the notion that it had serious claims to form an alternative government. Allusion has already been made to the ecclesiastical sanctuaries. At Beverley and at Durham especially, these remained lively institutions and incurred the corresponding dislike of Cromwell and the government. On the other hand, they enjoyed extreme popularity with the Pilgrims, who demanded their retention, together with that of ecclesiastical liberties in general. Alongside this archaism may be placed the demand for full-fledged benefit of clergy: 'a man to be saved by his book.' But a far more profoundly irrational element appears in the prevalence and influence of both false rumours and superstitious prophecies. The evidence for these bulks very large, yet since they do not figure in the official articles, their importance has been unduly minimized by modern historians. An age without mass-media of communication sounds attractive only until subjected to realistic scrutiny. In Tudor England the wildest rumours flew uncorrected, and tavern-talk was riddled with picturesque political folklore. On the eve of the Pilgrimage it was confidently reported that the King was about to confiscate Church plate and replace it with brass; that all gold was to be taken to the mint for re-testing at its owner's expense; that parish churches were to be at least five miles apart and, where they stood nearer, would be pulled down; that a tax was to be levied on horned cattle; that all baptisms, marriages and burials would be taxed; that no poor man would be allowed to eat white bread, goose, or capon without paying tax to the King, and that every man would be sworn to give his property and income, falsifiers of returns to lose all their goods. With equal wildness, every possible variety of rumour concerning the course of events and the King's intentions circulated during the rising.

As for the element of pseudo-historical prophecy concerning the fate of the King and the kingdom, it is known not only to have been widespread, but to have received some degree of credence even from educated men. Wilfrid Holme, a well-read Yorkshire squire who wrote a long metrical account of the Pilgrimage, devoted a large section of his work to such prophecies, yet he strove not so much to prove that prophecies were nonsensical, as to indicate that those spread by the Pilgrims could not possibly refer to the reign of Henry VIII. The depositions among the state-papers also make frequent reference to similar vaticinations. The majority of them obviously derive from the *Book of Merlin* by Geoffrey of Monmouth, whose credit as a prophet had been notably revived by the predicted accession of a Welshman to the throne. The most important of the Merlin-prophecies, *The Six Kings to follow King John,* a series of animal-parables, had long been applied to political struggles within the kingdom, especially by the Percy-Glendower faction opposing Henry IV. Now in 1536 all this farrago reappeared in force and attached itself to the predicted downfall of Henry VIII.

Despite its backward-looking and sometimes fantastic character, the Pilgrimage cannot justly be regarded as a merely negative episode in the development of Tudor England. It was constructive by reaction, since it forced the government to focus attention upon the North and to establish there an effective conciliar government. Yet the fact remains that only the King and his ministers could provide real solutions for its difficulties. A knot of feudal noblemen headed by the Percy interest and supported by Pole, Chapuys and the Habsburgs, promised as little for the future of Englishmen as did their successors of the next generation: Mary Stuart, Philip II, the Northern Earls and the conspirators against the life of Queen Elizabeth. In the event of military success, the Pilgrimage would inevitably have been called upon to provide constructive alternatives, a task which lay far beyond its apparent or conceivable capacity. It could neither have replaced the Tudors with another dynasty nor have served them by forming a tolerably stable and efficient government. Faced by the choice between Tudor conciliar policy and the brave, pious, but shortsighted Darcy with his eight thousand friends, his intrigues with Spain and Yorkism, what sane observer of our history could hesitate? But to the last Lord Darcy remained fortunate upon the page of history. It was he who at his examination issued those spirited words of defiance. 'Cromwell, it is thou that art the very original and chief causer of all this rebellion and mischief, and art likewise causer of the apprehension of us that be noblemen, and dost earnestly travail to bring us to one end and to strike off our heads, and I trust that ere thou die, though thou wouldst procure all the noblemen's heads within the realm to be stricken off, yet shall there one head remain that shall strike off thy head.' Nothing in Lord Darcy's eventful life became him like the leaving of it, and one fancies that these prophetic words must have re-echoed in Cromwell's mind three years later, when he himself lay under the shadow. For all that, Darcy was wrong. The cause of his adversary represented something enormously more positive than the mere destruction of the nobles. Men of Darcy's stamp were opposing forces far more formidable than a middle-class minister with a tenuous hold upon the royal favours. They were swimming directly against that stream which bore our nation to far higher destinies than any it had attained in the age of neo-feudalism.

If Cromwell, as his critics imagine, enmeshed England in a net of espionage, he failed to create one remotely comparable in efficiency with that of his successor Walsingham. The critics also fail to explain how a turbulent country without police-forces and detectives could be governed, save at least by instilling the principle that treasonable activities must be instantly reported. With Chapuys at the centre of the web, problems not dissimilar to those facing Walsingham soon developed. No foreign ambassador lured more discontented, obtuse and irresolute Englishmen to their deaths. The tentacles of Chapuys extended not merely to the North, but through the Home Counties, down to Devonshire and Cornwall, the Marches and Wales. His chief contact in the last was George Neville, Lord Abergavenny, veteran of the Wars of the Roses, an aggrieved son-in-law of the executed Duke of Buckingham and a friend of Queen Katherine. This nobleman's death in 1535 may well be regarded as the chief reason why the marcher lords and gentry did not join the North in the following year. 'I am sorry the Lord Abergavenny is dead', said Lord Montague; 'for if he were alive, he were able to make ten thousand men'. In Wales itself Rhys ap Griffith had suffered hanging as early as 1531, being the first of Katherine's supporters to die.

His uncle, the more formidable Sir James Griffith ap Howell, spent some time in prison and then became a stormy petrel along the Celtic fringe. In 1533 he was in Scotland; in 1534 he sent Chapuys information about the Fitzgerald rebellion from Ireland; in 1535 he had retired to the Continent. The undertaking of Sir James to raise Wales induced Chapuys for a time to place more reliance upon a western rising than upon one in the North. Though the Scottish threat made the North by far the more formidable military area, a rising in Wales and the Marches under the right leadership in 1536 would gravely have deepened the peril of the dynasty. The society of the farther western areas in general bore some resemblances to that of the North : its local loyalties, its widespread religious conservatism, economic grievances, rumours and prophecies all show parallels with those which preceded and accompanied the Pilgrimage of Grace. Nevertheless, in Devon and Cornwall the vast majority of the gentry and townsmen had thrown in their lot with the Tudors; compared with those of the North, feudal ties had become very weak, and it remains doubtful whether any magnate, whatever his resolution, could have staged a large-scale revolt.

Because of its spectacular outcome, the so-called Exeter Conspiracy has attained more than its due share of attention. Henry Courtenay, Marquis of Exeter and Earl of Devon, shared with the Poles an unenviable descent from the House of York : through his mother the Princess Katherine he was a grandson of Edward IV. Nevertheless, his cousin Henry VIII, having reversed the attainder placed upon Courtenay's father during the previous reign, accepted the young Marquis amongst his most intimate associates. Western offices were showered upon him, and for many years he had led an idyllic and pleasure-loving existence, apparently devoid of strong political interests. In 1531 he fell into rather serious trouble through the indiscretions of one of his gentlemen, but after a period of banishment from court, the old relationship appeared to be restored. Exeter had the misfortune, however, to marry a daughter of Queen Katherine's former chamberlain, William Blount, Lord Mountjoy; she proved a devout but indiscreet woman, mingling with the admirers of the Nun of Kent and involving herself in highly dubious communications with Chapuys. The King, sensing the restiveness of the Exeters and their friends, warned them clearly that they 'must not trip or vary for fear of losing their heads'. With them were linked the Blount connection, Sir Edward Neville, brother of Lord Abergavenny, a very few western gentry and, above all, their Yorkist kinsfolk, the mother and brothers of Reginald Pole: Lord Montague, who had married Abergavenny's daughter, and Sir Geoffrey Pole. The narrowing intimacy of the Courtenays, Poles and Nevilles, all families which needed to tread with the utmost circumspection, was in itself a folly of the first order. Yet all these aristocrats formed a loose-knit and ineffective group, adept at nothing save hating Cromwell and attracting the suspicions of the King. The Pilgrimage of Grace presented them with their one hope of successful reaction. The Marquis merely gave vent to such remarks as 'Knaves rule about the King. I trust to give them a buffet one day', yet he was too exclusive to see salvation in a rising led by inferiors like Robert Aske. No doubt he also reflected that the success of the northern rising was unlikely to put him personally into control of the State. He thus remained loyal and even presided at the trial of Darcy and Hussey.

Nevertheless, during these years he continued to provoke distrust by interrupting the levy of the subsidy in Devon and by causing the judges to report that he habitually coerced local juries into favouring his adherents. Though the details are unreliably reported, it seems also certain that his personal relations with Cromwell had become strained, though he masked his feelings sufficiently to preside at Cromwell's installation in 1537 as a Knight of the Garter. In the strict sense of the term, there was no Exeter Conspiracy, but merely a group of disloyal aristocrats and their adherents who talked treason with Chapuys and among themselves, sang political songs, and wanted a complete change of policy and personnel in the government. None had the drive, the courage and the backing from western popular opinion which an appeal to the sword would have demanded. When Exeter's enemies charged him with plotting the King's murder in order to seize the Crown for himself, they can scarcely have believed in the truth of their statements: such an action would have been intrinsically irrational, since the adherents of the Princess Mary formed the major section of the reactionary party upon which he would have been bound to rely.

In the summer of 1538 informers in and around the Pole household were reporting on the family's suspicious activities, especially on their correspondence with the exiled Reginald. Lord

Montague and his brother covered their tracks as best they could by burning their letters, but in October the unstable Sir Geoffrey, worked upon assiduously by the Earl of Southampton, confessed all he knew about himself and the rest of the circle. The disreputable brother consummated the family disaster which the high-principled brother had prepared. Though Geoffrey, at the price of infinite remorse, saved his own neck, he appears, both in his dealing with Chapuys and with Reginald, to have been by far the most guilty. Against Exeter, Montague and Sir Edward Neville, there was little to bring save evidence of mere verbal treasons under the new Act. And while this harsh instrument easily sufficed to convict the latter two, the Crown-lawyers were hard put to it to frame colourable charges against Exeter; they even resurrected as make-weights the old allegations of 1531. By this stage, however, subservient juries could be relied upon to take the darkest view of eminent suspects. Exeter, Montague, Neville and three of their adherents were executed in December. The aged Countess of Salisbury, mother of the Poles and a staunch friend of Katherine, was imprisoned, though only the flimsiest evidences of treason could be found against her. In 1541—the year after Cromwell's own death—she was to be brought out for butchery after the discovery of a further northern plot. With apparently no greater justice, Sir Nicholas Carew, a close friend of the Exeters, also suffered execution early in 1539, and Henry even troubled to take back from Lady Carew the 'most beautiful diamonds and pearls' which he had given her in happier days.

He had now come near fulfilling the threat once made to the French ambassador that he would make a clean sweep of the house of the White Rose. Little popular sympathy was shown to the victims either in the West Country or elsewhere; in general, public opinion believed in their complete guilt. The charge 'judicial murder' can perhaps rightly be used in relation to the Countess of Salisbury and to Carew: in regard to the others it needs some qualifications. Of the King's indiscriminate anger there can be no question: as it now seems, he could have afforded to be more generous with these foolish people. On the other hand, the emergency of State remained genuine enough. At this stage the government was concerned to prevent at all costs a repetition of the Pilgrimage of Grace; it was also frightened by the Truce of Nice, which appeared to presage joint invasion-attempts by France and Spain. And if there was no real Exeter Conspiracy, the whole network of treasonable and semi-treasonable activities had reached terrifying proportions. The friendships of Chapuys extended well beyond these northern and western groups. He felt sure of armed support from numerous distinguished men in the Home Counties and the south-east: the Earl of Rutland, Sir William Kingston, constable of the Tower, Sir Thomas Burgoyne, another son-in-law of the ill-fated Buckingham, Sir Thomas Elyot, late ambassador to Charles V, and particularly Lord Edmund Bray, who told Chapuys that over twenty peers and a hundred knights in districts not far from London stood ready to rise at short notice. Hopes extended towards possible disaffection on the part of even bigger men. The Duke of Norfolk himself was known equally to detest Cromwell and all prospects of religious innovation; the Duke of Suffolk, Henry's former brother-in-law and closest friend, had allied himself in marriage with the conservative Willoughbys; the Earl of Shrewsbury, chief magnate of the West Midlands, had expressed disapproval of certain aspects of the royal policy. Even allowing for these absurdly sanguine expectations of Chapuys, the foundations of the dynasty seemed exceptionally insecure in 1536–8. Against this sombre background at home and abroad must be viewed the Statute of Treasonable Words and its oppressive use not only against the guilty, but also against a few people who were not in fact among the more dangerous in the realm.

In the attack upon the Exeter group, Cromwell was no more concerned than a number of other ministers, and less closely concerned than Southampton. On the other hand, he had strong personal motives for wanting to see its liquidation. As events showed, he had far more to fear from a palace-revolution organized by a group of conservative nobles than from any rebellion. Any remaining illusions as to the fate which awaited him if one of these groups got the ear of the King had been dispelled by several of their members from Darcy to Exeter himself. When he read Pole's book he threatened with a most unusual access of anger that he would make its author 'eat his own heart', and not long afterwards he wrote to one of Pole's servants, 'Pity it is, that the folly of one brainsick Poole, or to say better, of one witless fool, should be the ruin of so great a family'. It is both nonsensical and unjust to the King and to his ministers to regard the attack on the Exeters and Poles as simply an act of revenge against Reginald. It was very much more. Yet if revengeful motives seem in general to have been foreign to the impassive temperament of Cromwell, it looks as if, on this occasion at least, he experienced the darker emotions.

In Chapuys sedition had a devoted organizer; its weakness lay in the fact that it lacked a head. From time to time, he made various suggestions, including Reginald Pole himself, towards an alternative to the unsatisfactory incumbent of the throne, but so long as Queen Katherine lived he was compelled to see her and her daughter Mary as the true keys to the situation. It was not for lack of opportunity that Katherine refused to respond to his overtures and to place herself at the head of armed rebellion. Had she appealed to Pope and Emperor in 1535, they would no doubt have done far more to provoke and assist such a reaction. Yet to the last Katherine remained a true Queen of England and a true wife: she would be no party to what she regarded as the sin of rebellion, or seek to profit from her husband's overthrow and death. To few of her queens has England's historical debt proved greater, for in the time of her personal calamity she held our fate in her hands and guarded it well. Katherine died in the first days of 1536, some months before the supreme crisis; and her last act was to write the King a letter vowing her love and her earnest regard for his spiritual welfare.

The Supreme Head remained unregenerate. Chapuys describes how, dressed in yellow from top to toe with a white feather in his cap, he gave a ball at Greenwich and circulated among the guests with the baby Elizabeth in his arms, saying, 'God be praised; the old harridan is dead, now there is no fear of war'. One feels no difficulty in believing the story, though it may lose nothing in the telling by this talented *raconteur*. Certainly the mischievous ambassador proceeded to write many letters in an attempt to convince the Emperor that Henry had poisoned his former wife. Within a few months Chapuys saw with delight Anne Boleyn go to the block; then, with growing depression, the collapse of the Pilgrimage and the steady failure of his blue-blooded English friends to roll back the march of history. He was yet destined to long years in England; having survived Cromwell, he reconciled himself somewhat to events, and accorded a grudging respect to the bloated but still regal occupant of the throne. His personal anticlimax was by no means the only one to mark the post-Cromwellian years.

Chapter Seven

Cromwell and the English Bible

IMMENSELY the most important of Cromwell's contributions to English religious history was the printing and dissemination of bibles in the English tongue. Behind this momentous step, the political agency was that of Cromwell, while the work of translation was that of the radical English Lutherans. Only hardened ecclesiasts will believe that Gardiner and the conservative English bishops would ever have done this work willingly, done it as well, or indeed done it at all. Yet towards their patent opposition only bigots will be unduly censorious, for no gift proved itself so explosive, so incalculable in its effects upon Church and State. For what it is worth, the overwhelming consensus of subsequent English opinion would not have had history changed. Any regrets would have been self-accusations, since the vernacular Bible soon became central to our culture, so to remain at least until the twentieth century. Here for once the cant phrases contain much truth: no book ever played a more creative part in moulding the virtues and in cloaking the sins of a nation which soon begat like-minded offspring across the oceans.

One may believe or disbelieve John Foxe's story that Cromwell memorized the whole of Erasmus's New Testament during his journey to and from Rome. If he did so, his motives may have been linguistic or pelmanistic rather than devotional; perhaps this was the stage at which he was brushing up a meagre education in Latin. Nevertheless, he could doubtless boast a far better knowledge of the Bible than most contemporary laymen, and there remain abundant signs of his lively interest in the early vernacular translations and translators. His connections with Coverdale, destined to become the principal agent of this task, go back at least five years before his appointment as chief minister. As an Augustinian friar at Cambridge, Coverdale sent Cromwell some gossip from that place in a letter of 27 August, 1527, saying that he would have been delighted to come to London had he known Cromwell so desired. Another letter, dated merely 'from the Augustines this May Day', is wrongly assigned by the *Letters and Papers of Henry VIII* to the year 1531; it is signed 'frere Myles Coverdale' and cannot be later than 1527, since in the subsequent year Coverdale threw off his friar's coat, preached Protestantism and fled abroad. In this second letter he reminds Cromwell of 'the godly communication' he had had with him 'in master Moorys house upon Easter eve', and he then descants upon his great need of books. 'Now I begin to taste of holy scriptures; now, honour be to God, I am set to the most sweet smell of holy letters, with the godly savour of holy and ancient doctors, unto whose knowledge I cannot attain without diversity of books, as is not unknown to your most excellent wisdom. Nothing in the world I desire but books as concerning my learning. They once had, I do not doubt but almighty God shall perform that in me which He, of His most plentiful favour and grace, hath begun.' On the strength of these remarks, it has been suggested that Coverdale was already preparing, under the patronage of Cromwell and Sir Thomas More, for his translation of the Bible. It seems—whatever the shocked Gairdner may have thought—very possible that his reference is indeed to Sir Thomas More; if so, what a fascinating conjuncture of three diverse and remarkable men it reveals! All the same, the letter says nothing about actual translation, and if we accept Coverdale's later statements literally, he did not begin translating until 1534, when he was abroad and under the patronage of Jacob van Meteren, a merchant of Antwerp.

Before this stage, Cromwell had made contact with that earlier and more formidable translator, William Tyndale. Though in May 1530 Tyndale had been denounced as a heretic and perverter of God's word, less than a year later the King was considering the possibility of enlisting his pen. Henry was no doubt deeply impressed by Tyndale's extremist erastianism, as revealed in *The Obedience of a Christian Man*. Cromwell accordingly wrote to Stephen Vaughan in the Netherlands with an order to search for Tyndale and induce him to return to England. In January 1531, Vaughan sent a double reply to the King and to Cromwell, reporting Tyndale's answer that the news of recent events in England—no doubt he meant persecutions by the bishops—had made him afraid to return. The version sent to Cromwell has a confidential postscript showing that Vaughan had been deeply impressed by Tyndale and had become ardent to procure his return. 'Would God he were in England!' In March 1531 Vaughan wrote again to Cromwell in the same strain; in April he reported to the King that he had actually interviewed Tyndale in a field outside Antwerp, and he now enclosed a manuscript copy of Tyndale's *Answer* to Sir Thomas More. The royal perusal of this work occasioned precisely the reverse of the effect intended by the naïve Vaughan. The King, now seeing Tyndale as an opinionated heretic, peremptorily told Cromwell to make Vaughan cease his attempts. 'Wherefore, Stephen,' writes Cromwell, 'I heartily pray you that from henceforth in all your doings and proceedings and writing to the King's Highness, ye do justly, truly and unfeignedly show yourself to be no fautor unto the said Tyndale ne to his works . . . but rather utterly to contemn and abhor the same.' His majesty is still benignly inclined to Vaughan, yet if the latter persists, he may easily incur the royal indignation. Few of Cromwell's letter-drafts bear as many corrections as this, and it has been assumed that he wrote in extreme perturbation after the King's display of wrath, or else that his first draft was not bitter enough to please the King, who made him strengthen it. In fact, the corrected version is not notably harsher than the original, while Vaughan's reply shows that Cromwell had added a postscript authorizing Vaughan to contact Tyndale afresh and persuade him to submit to the King's mercy. In the event, Vaughan had two further interviews with Tyndale, which he reported during May and June in letters both to Henry and to the minister. On the first occasion Tyndale magnanimously offered to return and submit to any punishment, provided only that the King would set forth a bare text of the Scriptures, translated by any person whatever. Even as late as November, Vaughan again wrote on Tyndale's behalf to Cromwell, but the latter, no doubt conscious of the risks involved when the King's sensitive conscience began to operate, seems prudently to have dropped the matter. Tyndale never returned to England. In 1536 he was tempted by an English betrayer to leave the protection of the English House in Antwerp, seized, condemned for heresy, and strangled before his body was consigned to the flames.

In 1530 the King had proclaimed that it was unnecessary for the scripture to be in the English tongue and in the hands of the common people, though he professed himself ready to consider the possibility of a translation 'by great, learned and Catholic persons'. Since then, the atmosphere had changed. In December 1534 the Convocation of Canterbury under Cranmer petitioned the King to decree a translation. Coverdale had meanwhile begun his task; working with extraordinary speed, he had it printed by October 1535. In his dedication to the King he claimed to have made his translation 'out of five sundry interpreters', since identified as Tyndale, Luther, the Vulgate, Pagninus (the Italian Dominican who had made a good literal Latin version of the Old Testament from the Hebrew) and the Zürich version of 1531.

The limitations of Coverdale's work have often been remarked. He could make no pretences to direct translation from Hebrew. His vocabulary was too often impregnated by Germanisms like 'deadoffering' (*todopfer*) and 'let himself (*liess sich*) be shaven'. Throughout the New Testament he did little to improve upon Tyndale's work of genius, and in the extreme instance of the Epistle of St. James, with its 108 verses, he changed only three words. His achievement remains impressive. This was the first complete English Bible to appear in print, since three-quarters of the Old Testament had not been produced by Tyndale. Again, Coverdale excels in the felicity of his phrasing, in a new smoothness, a sense for the musical qualities of a sentence. It is significant that in 1662 his rendering of the Psalms was preferred even to that of the Authorized Version by the revisers of the Book of Common Prayer: it is the text still used for liturgical purposes by the Church of England.

Parts of this Bible were being brought to England by the end of August 1535, when the Southwark printer James Nicholson (a Netherlander by origin and formerly a glazier) solicited Cromwell's support for its publication in England under the royal privilege. His letter shows that Nicholson himself took the initial risks, but that he felt confident of Cromwell's assistance. 'And as your goodness ever and only hath put your foot for the preferment of God's word: even so that your mastership will now set to your helping hands that the whole Bible may come forth, whereof as much as is yet come into England I have sent unto you by this bringer George Constantine a copy.' If Cromwell obtains this sanction, continues Nicholson, England will be more in debt to him than to St. Augustine himself. The printer's hopes were fulfilled with great expedition. Prompted by Cromwell, the King handed the translation to Gardiner and other bishops. According to a not improbable anecdote related by William Fulke in 1583, the prelates answered that it contained many faults. Well, replied Henry, but are there any heresies maintained thereby? When the bishops replied that they could find none, the royal order was immediately given. 'If there be no heresies, then in God's name let it go abroad among our people.'

Why did Henry, so bitter a critic of Tyndale, fall so readily to the blandishments of a translation made by another of his exiled Lutheran subjects? A considerable number of facts and statements combine to show the strength of the influence brought to bear by Anne Boleyn, who maintained during the brief period of her ascendancy a more genuinely personal interest in the vernacular Bible than her detractors have allowed. Again, the Coverdale version presented a proposition very different from those of Tyndale, since it contained a flattering dedication to the King and was not loaded with overt and trenchant Lutheran propaganda. As for Cromwell, he had become deeply implicated in the plan from the time he received Nicholson's letter. As Vicegerent he issued two sets of ecclesiastical injunctions in September 1536 and September 1538; while everyone knows that the latter caused English bibles to be set up in churches, it is seldom realized that the first version of the 1536 injunctions already made this command. There survive three copies of this version by the royal printer Berthelet; it orders that every parson must provide by the following 1 August a book of the whole Bible, both in Latin and also in English, 'and lay the same in the choir for every man that will to look and read thereon'. The clergy shall discourage no man from reading any part of the Bible, 'but rather comfort, exhort and admonish every man to read the same as the very word of God and the spiritual food of man's soul'. On the other hand, the laity must be gently and charitably exhorted that 'they do in no wise stiffly or eagerly contend or strive one with another about the same', but refer controversial points to the judgement of those better learned. These copies of the injunctions were printed about the middle of July 1536, but seem to have been conceived much earlier. In the previous May, Queen Anne had been executed, and by the summer Cromwell perhaps thought it unwise to press on with a scheme she had been supporting. Whatever his motives, he withdrew this particular injunction and left Coverdale's Bible to be sold privately. It evidently met with immediate success, since in 1537 the enterprising James Nicholson himself reprinted it in two revised editions.

By this time Nicholson was confronted by a formidable competitor in the so-called Matthew Bible, edited in reality by John Rogers, then chaplain to the English House at Antwerp, who prudently adapted the pseudonym Thomas Matthew. This version was first read by Cranmer and brought by him on 4 August 1537 to Cromwell's notice. With his usual promptitude, Cromwell took a copy to the King, who permitted it to be bought and read in the kingdom. By 13 August Cranmer wrote to thank Cromwell for his pains. 'You have showed me more pleasure herein than if you had given me a thousand pound, and I doubt not but that hereby such fruit of good knowledge shall ensue, that it shall well appear hereafter, what high and acceptable service you have done unto God and the King, which shall so much redound to your honour that, besides God's reward, you shall attain perpetual memory for the same within this realm. And as for me, you may reckon me your bondman for the same, and I dare be bold to say, so may ye do my lord of Worcester' (i.e. Latimer). Needless to insist, the version which commanded such phrases was also a distinctly Protestant presentation. Rogers had worked intimately with both Tyndale and Coverdale; he afterwards became a close associate of Melanchthon and held office as superintendent of the Lutheran church at Dietmarsch. In course of time, he was to become one of the first martyrs of the Marian persecution. Though a fine stylist and a sound scholar with a knowledge of Greek and Hebrew, he closely followed his predecessors, especially Tyndale, whom he preferred wherever possible to Coverdale. In the Old Testament particularly, Rogers made considerable use of two French translators. One of them was the elderly and eminent Lefèvre of Etaples, who had followed and even anticipated many Lutheran teachings, yet never broke with Rome. The other was Olivetan of Noyon, Calvin's kinsman and early inspirer, whose French translation had appeared in 1535 under Waldensian patronage. To the text Rogers added over two thousand notes, more peaceable and moderate in tone than those of Tyndale, yet owing a substantial debt to Oecolampadius and other Lutheran scholars.

Cromwell's connections with the Matthew Bible did not cease with its arrival upon the market. Its publisher was that characteristic figure of our early Reformation, Richard Grafton, a grocer of London and a merchant adventurer of Antwerp. Knowing whence favours might come, he sent Cromwell six copies and received the payment of ten pounds. Fearing piracy by his rivals he then pestered Cromwell to licence the version under his privy seal, and to forbid any other publisher to reprint it for three years. Failing this support, he continued, would Cromwell please order every parish priest to buy a copy and every abbey six copies? His business letters, their acumen plentifully interlarded with godly phrases, read little to our modern taste, but we need not for a moment doubt Grafton's evangelical sincerity. Biblical publishers were then understandably worried men; they were compelled to invest large sums in risky enterprises beset both by powerful conservative enemies and by trade-rivals uninhibited by modern laws of copyright. The hard facts of the situation ensured that their motives must be mixed. The *naïveté* of these early Protestants appears more pointedly in Grafton's argument that the dissemination of bibles would put a stop to the religious disputes then rife in the realm!

Placed between the rivals Nicholson and Grafton, Cromwell did the fair thing by both of them. He gratified the former by licensing his Coverdale Bible, as he had now licensed Grafton's Matthew Bible. Yet the fact that no private edition of the Matthew Bible appeared may well be due to prohibitory hints or orders issued by Cromwell to other publishers. While he did not, as Grafton urged, force the clergy and the monasteries to purchase the Matthew Bible, he spurred on the bishops to force some sort of Bible upon the parishes, hence benefiting both Nicholson and Grafton, who were now competing on even terms within an enlarged official market. Already in the autumn of 1537 Latimer ordered every clerk in his diocese to obtain by Christmas a bible, or at least a New Testament, in Latin and English, and to read a chapter a day. At the beginning of 1538 a royal proclamation commanded the justices of the peace to see that the clergy preached the word of God sincerely and truly, and that they suffered the people to have the English Bible. In the subsequent months several bishops, even some of known conservative views, like Vesey of Exeter and Lee of York, issued corresponding injunctions. Alongside Cranmer and Latimer, Bishop Shaxton of Salisbury led the Reforming group and gave especially detailed directions. In this diocese, clerics with benefices valued at ten pounds or more were commanded to buy the whole Bible, while the poorer ones might rest content with a New Testament. All must read a chapter a day and learn by heart a chapter a fortnight. Shaxton urged, though he could not yet order, every parish to buy an English bible from its church funds, or from money formerly given to maintain lights before images; this copy must be chained to a desk in the nave, 'where he that is lettered may read, and other unlearned may hear wholesome doctrine and comfort to their souls'. A circular letter written by Cromwell to some or all of the bishops about the spring of 1538 indicates the degree of pressure he was bringing to bear in this same direction. He hears that the King's ordinances are being remissly observed in the dioceses and commands the bishops to lay forth the English Bible openly in their houses. The parsons and vicars must be made to provide copies at their own cost for the parish churches, so that every man by free access to them may be the more apt to understand sermons or scripture and to instruct his family at home. In addition, the bishops must make their clergy exhort the laity to read the Bible in the spirit of an instruction which Cromwell is enclosing: this instruction is to be sent out to every parish priest, together with a date, appointed by the bishop, before which the English Bible must be laid forth in every church. No particular edition was prescribed, and hence, under this purposeful directive, the existing editions of both the cheaper Coverdale Bible and the dearer but better Matthew Bible were no doubt rapidly exhausted. Immediate and general compliance with this order should not, of course, be assumed. It is known, for example, from visitation records of the Lincoln diocese that in the autumn of 1539 many churches still lacked bibles, either because copies had become unobtainable, or because of slackness, apathy and distaste on the lower levels.

For some time, Cromwell had been planning an authoritative edition of the English Bible. Early in 1538 he decided to entrust the revision to the safe, moderate Coverdale, and the printing to Grafton and his partner Whitchurch. These latter were men of standing, and may have been known to control more capital than Nicholson, or other possible publishers. In the event, the making of this Great Bible was attended by some sensational developments. On technical grounds, the Vicegerent chose Paris as the place of printing, since, in his own words to the French ambassador, 'printing is finer there than elsewhere, and with the great number of printers and abundance of paper, books are dispatched sooner than in any other country'. As he was to learn, there were also circumstances of a less favourable sort. At the request of Henry VIII, King Francis licensed Grafton and Whitchurch to print the Bible both in Latin and in English with any printer in France, and to transport it to England, provided it contained no 'private or unlawful opinions'. The partners consequently transferred to Paris, where they lodged with their printer Regnault, and on 23 June 1538, they wrote to tell Cromwell that they were 'entered into your work of the Bible' and to send him the first printed sheets. They intended to print two copies on vellum, one for the King, one for Cromwell: they are probably the two now surviving at St. John's College, Cambridge, and in the National Library of Wales. Already at this date, Grafton and Whitchurch asked for any financial help Cromwell could give them; they also feared danger from the papists and begged Cromwell to defend them by sending letters to the English ambassador in Paris. Ironically enough, the latter was Bishop Gardiner. In August and September further letters report steady progress. In October Edmund Bonner had replaced Gardiner at the embassy and reported 'a stay made at Paris touching the printing of the Bible in English'. On 13 December the publishers were trying to send Cromwell some of the printed sheets through Bonner, but four days later the blow fell when the Inquisitor-General of France forbade the continuance of the work and summoned Regnault before him. Grafton and Whitchurch, glad to escape, fled to England. On 31 December Cromwell told the French ambassador that he had personally sunk £400 in the enterprise. The book, he argued, could not possibly spread heresy in France, since its text was a mere word-for-word translation to help Englishmen who knew no Latin. He besought the King of France to allow the printing to continue, or at least to agree that the unfinished books should be sent into England. After much delay and palaver, the presses, type and workmen of Regnault were permitted in February 1539 to be transferred to England, where the work was duly completed. On his return to Paris, Grafton succeeded in salvaging four great vats of printed sheets, which a corrupt French official had quietly sold to a haberdasher for lining caps, instead of obeying the Inquisitor and consigning them to the flames in the Place Maubert.

The suggestion was made by A. W. Pollard that the French

intervention was political rather than theological in purpose, but this notion is thoroughly disproved by contemporary evidence, which also reveals pressure arising from Rome and from English conservatives anxious to interrupt the printing in Paris. Foxe blames Gardiner for secretly backing the attempt to destroy the Great Bible, but here one expects violent prejudice and fails to find any solid support for the assertion. After Cromwell's time, it is true, Gardiner tried to get the Great Bible rescinded. As for Bonner, he apparently did all in his power to help Grafton recover what he could from the *débâcle*. Whatever Bonner's reactionary zeal in later years, Foxe's jaundiced view that he was guilty of duplicity during these exchanges cannot be maintained, for he was at this time a zealous Cromwellian who freely acknowledged that he owed everything to the minister. Not only did he show himself the dutiful ambassador, but as bishop of London he hastened to place six copies of the Great Bible in St. Paul's, and was among the first bishops to order that the Epistle and Gospel should be read at high mass in English. On the other hand, it is difficult to comprehend the minds of those ecclesiasts who attempt to depict the conservative majority of the bishops as burning with zeal to translate the Bible, yet mysteriously prevented by sinister forces. Occupied by heavy duties, deterred by a perfectly intelligible caution and worldly wisdom, anxious to wrap up explosive controversial words in Latinized wadding derived from the Vulgate, they were the last agents to undertake the task. For good or ill, the early history of the English Bible derives from the militant Protestants and from their political backer Cromwell. We cannot at once blame them for the controversies they aroused and deny them the initiative in a great experiment. Even the role played by Cranmer in this act of the drama seems a little ambiguous and confused. His sense of the urgent desirability of a good translation and his active support for the Matthew Bible cannot be questioned, but even here he seemed curiously unaware that it derived overwhelmingly from Tyndale, who had been condemned as a heretic after Cranmer's own promotion to the see of Canterbury. Again, his plan to divide out the translating of the New Testament between ten bishops of uneven scholarship, and still more uneven doctrinal partisanship, would generally be described as unintelligent had it come from a lesser man. This point was granted even by Canon Maynard Smith, whose reverence for the bishops and dislike of

Cromwell led him into some inaccuracies and underestimates regarding Cromwell's share in the Great Bible.

The first edition of the latter was completed in April 1539, but some substantial changes appear in that of April 1540, which, furnished with a preface by Cranmer, became the standard. Before the end of 1541 no less than seven editions had been published. Cromwell's own further dealings with the project were highly necessary to maintain the just interests of the publishers. In November 1539 Cranmer wrote that Berthelet and Whitchurch had paid him a visit and stressed the heavy cost of publication. Berthelet was not a partner of the firm, but probably attended as an independent expert to advise Cranmer. On his advice, the Archbishop wished to fix the selling price at 13s. 4d., but Whitchurch had told him that Cromwell would prefer ten shillings. The publishers thought this latter price low, but would accept it, provided Cromwell would grant them a monopoly. The minister did the next best thing and immediately obtained a patent from the King forbidding any printer to print an English Bible for the next five years, unless deputed by himself. There is no evidence that he used this monopoly for personal profit: in fact, in April 1540 he allowed Berthelet to print an edition independently of Grafton.

The character of the Great Bible certainly justified Cromwell's choice of his former associate Coverdale. As his basis, the latter took the Matthew Bible, which was a compound of his own earlier work and, to a larger extent, that of Tyndale. This he corrected with the aid of two very sound guides: Sebastian Munster's edition of the Hebrew Old Testament, published along with a Latin translation in 1535; and the New Testament of Erasmus. The chief innovation was intended to placate the Catholic addiction to the Vulgate. Where the latter added anything to the Hebrew or Greek text, Coverdale now inserted the addition in smaller type and in brackets. This very significant step cannot have been taken except by Cromwell's consent: it may well represent an original suggestion from the minister, since Coverdale himself was well aware of the small authority possessed by these additions and cannot have welcomed them, either as a Protestant or as a scholar. Cromwell himself had a statesman's awareness of the gratuitous offence given by Tyndale's and Rogers' presentations of the Scriptures. Their prologues and notes were calculated to alienate conservative opinion, and a Bible which repelled a section of the nation could not possibly play the exalted part within the State-Church for which he had cast it. In the event, the mature methods of Coverdale were admirably adapted to an 'official' version. Though he continued in the Great Bible to reject such words as 'church', 'priest' (for a Christian minister), 'charity' and 'penance', he also avoided some of the expressions which had aroused Catholic feeling. In general, his work is sober, exact and restrained, toning down at some sacrifice of vividness the asperities and inconsistencies of Tyndale.

To assess the ultimate results of all these versions would lead us far beyond our present subject. No English Bible, however carefully presented, led to any immediate or easily-won spirit of charity. On the one hand, we soon encounter fanatical Protestants who would not stop reading the Bible aloud in church, even during service-time. On the other, we find Queen Mary's government burning copies of the Great Bible, trying to roll back the years and withdraw the English scriptures from the laity. Again, according to that able but noisy Protestant Thomas Becon, in many parishes the laity remained quite apathetic in these matters, 'so little pleasure have these filthy swine and currish dogs in that most sweet and singular treasure'. Yet it is of the nature of all such stories to represent the exceptional : concerning the quiet and steady mental processes at work throughout England during the two decades which followed official acceptance of the English Bible, records are largely and inevitably silent. In view of the outcome, there can be little doubt that the Great Bible played a major part in the gradual permeation of English society by scriptural habits of mind. What Cromwell persuaded the King to give could not be effectively withdrawn by any successor, even by Church and State acting in conjunction. Of the rivers which England crossed during the momentous years of Cromwell's ministry, this one seems in retrospect the widest and deepest of all.

The remainder of Cromwell's biblical activities may be briefly recounted. Some time in the year 1539 there appeared yet another translation : that of the barrister Richard Taverner. Details regarding its backers are unknown, yet since the translator was among the most vigorous of Cromwell's team of pamphleteers, and since the publisher Thomas Berthelet was the King's printer, the work must have proceeded with the full allowance, and probably with the active support, of the Vicegerent. Like the Great Bible, Taverner's version provides a revision of Matthew, though one of a much less painstaking character. Taverner knew no Hebrew, but he was a good Greek scholar, adhering so literally to the Greek text that he sometimes fell into obscurities. He did not, however, lack literary initiative and often invented expressions which found their way at last into the Authorized Version. Taverner himself was a thoroughgoing Lutheran, and it may have been at Cromwell's request that he omitted Tyndale's prologue to *Romans* and other ultra-radical embellishments which had remained in the Matthew version.

Though Archbishop Cranmer's contributions cannot be regarded as of pre-eminent importance, a preface by him was submitted for Cromwell's approval and then placed in the various editions of the Great Bible from April 1540 onwards. In consequence, the latter often received, absurdly enough, the title 'Cranmer's Bible'. Yet the musical English and charitable spirit of this preface earned the many commendations since bestowed upon them. With a grace of style beyond the reach of his English contemporaries and a liberal foresight greater than that of his episcopal colleagues, the Archbishop takes a characteristically Anglican view of the function of the Bible. Most of the Scriptures, he urges, may be understood by simple men, since their authors wrote to instruct and not to indulge their own vainglory. Nevertheless, they contain hard passages, and from these the plain man is more likely to derive enlightenment by consulting his parish priest, or a preacher, than by propounding them for the subject of an ale-house wrangle. The popularity of this latter primrose path to scriptural knowledge had already attracted the attention of the government. By a proclamation of April 1539 no one except a beneficed man or university graduate was allowed to expound the Bible or to read it aloud in church. This month saw in fact the beginning of a strong conservative reaction unpalatable to Cromwell, but there is no proof of his own hostility to this not very oppressive safeguard. He cannot have shared the King's doctrinal alarm, but as a statesman he feared the internal disunity which arose from doctrinal strife and faction. In opening his last parliamentary session on 12 April 1540, he made a moving plea for a concord which should triumph on the one hand over the 'temerity and carnal liberty' of the gospellers and on the other over the 'inveterate corruption and superstitious obstinacy' of the conservatives. Hence arose quarrels and commotions most detestable to all good Christians. They called one another papist and heretic, miserably abusing the Holy Word of God which the King had permitted them to read in the vulgar tongue. They turned God's gift, now into heresy, now into superstition. The King favoured neither side, but professed the true faith of Christ. He desired to establish the rule of the Gospel, to separate pious from impious ceremonies and to eradicate disunity by enforcing penal laws. Cromwell then went on to announce Henry's plan to draw up the *Institution of a Christian Man*. This speech foreshadows in striking degree Henry's own much-vaunted last speech to Parliament. It had already become painfully obvious that, whatever its future advantages, free access to the Scriptures had failed to produce any immediate foretaste of Isaiah's millennium, when the wolf should dwell with the lamb and the lion eat straw like the ox.

Why did Cromwell show this pertinacious and creative furtherance of the vernacular Scriptures? His critics are as usual ready with their simple answers. 'His main object', writes an eminent clerical historian 'was to destroy the power of the clergy, and thought that the best way for doing so [*sic*] was to concentrate on the Bible rather than on the altar. Anyone could read an open Bible for himself, but no one but a priest could celebrate Mass.' This may well be a boomerang likely to hit the champions of medieval ecclesiasticism hardest. If mere Bible-reading helped to destroy certain types of clerical power, perhaps they were best destroyed. Even so, to the Church as understood in the later Middle Ages, the Bible presented two challenges. It pointed obvious contrasts between the intricate legal, coercive, liturgical, economic and architectural apparatus which the Church had developed, and, on the other hand, the unaffected simplicity which marked the lives of Jesus of Nazareth and the Apostles. Again, the Bible had much to say about the controls exercised by kings over a national religion, but it said extremely little about the Papacy and the bishops.

All this admitted, I find the merely secular and destructive Cromwell, the Biblical *saboteur*, a little too simple for the known facts. Must the unfortunate man never be allowed a motive outside the straight role assigned him by Gairdner's Tudor saga? One whose Biblical interests long antedated his power to turn them to political ends need not be denied a belief in the educative power of the Scriptures for a new type of Christian society. And if he really believed that the English Bible would finally destroy the influence of the priesthood, this must have been the greatest of all his miscalculations! Even in Cromwell's circle there were not wanting men like Sir Francis Bigod, who foresaw the new type of clergy which the Bible and the pulpit would produce. Evidence exists in plenty to show Cromwell's real dislike for the unscriptural accretions which had become so prominent in the medieval church; for men of his stamp this attitude was presumably based upon logic rather than upon sensibility. To change the basis of clerical authority, to maintain the momentum of reform and rationalization, to render impossible a reversal of the statutory changes: these ideas, or some very like them, must have occurred to so intelligent and incisive a mind, but it seems to me difficult to relegate them all to a purely political sphere. The whole essence of the situation lay in its lack of these neat 'religious' and 'political' categories. Cromwell was no theological innovator; despite his reputation as arch-heretic, he made no spectacular departures from orthodox doctrine. Even so, his sympathies lay with the near-Protestant Henricians such as Cranmer and Latimer, who stood decisively and disinterestedly for the policy of the open Bible. In Cromwell's mind, if I conjecture aright, the policy had some individual connotations. It was most likely related to his notions of efficiency in Church and State. And since Erasmus had come to dominate the educated minds of Euro᠎ :, an 'efficient' Church could not be wholly divorced from the concept of the Bible as educator of the common man.

Chapter Eight

The Dissolution

IN January 1535 a grandiloquent commission appointed Thomas Cromwell Vicegerent, Vicar General and Special Commissary to exercise all jurisdiction inherent in the Supreme Head of the English Church. It permitted him to appoint deputy-commissioners at will, gave him and them power to visit all ecclesiastical institutions, and make enquiry concerning the conduct of the clergy, 'even if they shine in archiepiscopal or episcopal splendours'. They might punish the culpable by deprivation, suspension or sequestration, control all synods, chapters and convocations, preside over the elections of prelates, cite and coerce all subjects of the realm in causes ecclesiastical, receive the surrenders of churches, and in general exercise the full plenitude of ecclesiastical power. This is an astonishing document; it enlarges even upon those grandiose papal commissions to Wolsey which seem to form its model. Cromwell's new titles, themselves borrowed from ecclesiastical usage, are employed rather loosely and interchangeably in subsequent documents; sometimes he is simply called Vicegerent.

The most immediate purpose of the commission was to empower its recipient to visit the religious houses, a partial suppression of which had been for some time adumbrated. As early as February 1532 a new-style secularization had been executed when the canons of Christ Church Aldgate, their finances in a hopeless muddle, surrendered to the King. The latter assumed their properties by statute and, unlike Wolsey in former years, made no pretence of devoting them to charitable and educational purposes. In March 1533 Chapuys understood Henry to say that he was determined, and bound by his coronation oath, to unite to the Crown all the goods which churchmen held of it. At this stage also, the small but reputable Observant Order defied the King and suffered dissolution. During 1534 Chapuys twice suggested the imminence of a more general attack; he even credited Cromwell with a plan for distributing ecclesiastical revenues amongst the gentry in order to gain their support. In the autumn parliamentary session, a scheme of unparalleled radicalism became the subject of memoranda now among the state-papers. It suggested a system of salaried bishops with their former temporalities transferred to the State; the King to have first-fruits, half the incomes of cathedrals and collegiate churches, and a third of every archdeaconry. Monasteries with less than thirteen inmates were scheduled for confiscation, while from the larger houses sums proportionate to the number of religious would be assigned to their upkeep, the surplus being presented to the King. The authors of the plan are unknown, but it was probably one of those accorded serious thought by Cromwell. Whatever its obvious merits as compared with that ultimately adopted, its political implications must have been considered too dangerous. It contravened the principle *divide et impera*. In particular, Cromwell cannot have relished the prospect of driving the hitherto compliant bishops into opposition, and thus introducing rancour into Parliament, where episcopal influence and voting-power retained importance. So far as the secular clergy were concerned, the safe step was not such a confiscation, but rather the exploitation of their large taxable capacity.

One cannot seriously question that the monastic dissolutions were primarily based upon the financial ambitions of the government. Those who thought more sentimentally than Cromwell may indeed have felt many other motives. To make other kings envy, admire and conceivably imitate England; these were thoughts which seem to have suggested themselves to Henry's mind. Cromwell himself had no love for monasticism. Here he typified both the merchant classes and the civil service: while we cannot, despite his dislike for incontinent priests, credit him with sensitive moral repulsions, his tidy, efficient mind was doubtless repelled by the ample measure of disciplinary and administrative chaos which struck all observers of the monastic scene and which had occupied so large a share of his own energies. In his version of Utopia, there can have been no place for monasticism. However elaborate the injunctions he issued on the eve of dissolution, he cannot have entertained serious schemes of monastic reform. The absence of any such schemes emanating from either clerics or laymen remains a striking feature of the last phase of English monastic history: it betokens a general discouragement extending far beyond men of Cromwellian outlook. Yet even in 1534, the new Royal Supremacy did not in itself necessarily demand a general dissolution of the monasteries. Whatever Romish inclinations were attributed by greedy or prejudiced enemies to the religious orders, they did not undergo suppression because of any special devotion or loyalty to the Holy See. Apart from the attitude of a few Carthusians and Observants, this was the last charge which could justly be brought against English monks as a whole. It is again tempting to detect in the dissolution a far-seeing plan to bind a great body of aristocratic and middle-class purchasers to the Crown, the Royal Supremacy and the new régime in Church and State. This notion, which certainly suggested itself not only to Chapuys but to some of the purchasers, cannot have escaped the mind of Thomas Cromwell. The latter stood in no position to forecast, even in his own mind, the amount of property which the Crown would need to alienate over future years in order to meet current necessities. Nevertheless, he allowed the alienation of an extremely small part of the monastic lands between 1536 and his fall, despite the unprecedented government-expenditure of those years. Nothing seems less likely than that he would have approved the reckless sales which marked the years 1543–7 and which may have accounted for almost two-thirds of the monastic lands.

From the time of Cromwell's entry, there existed every inducement to undertake a capital levy of heroic proportions in order both to meet short-term needs and to endow the Crown in permanency with the financial keys to strong government. Cromwell provided good management and began to acquire some departmental surpluses, but the economical days of Henry VII had gone beyond recall. The Reformation Parliament proved stingy with hard cash; the customs revenues were declining; military equipment was becoming more elaborate; inflation steadily increased the cost of fortifications, ships and palaces. In the year 1533 the northern marches cost the Crown nearly £25,000; in 1534 the Geraldine rebellion cost £38,000 more than the Irish Government could produce; in 1536 the Pilgrimage of Grace cost £50,000 to suppress, and in the following years the constant threat of invasion forced Cromwell to find very large sums for levies, fortifications and the Navy. In Tudor times the price of security was always higher than Englishmen were prepared to admit and never more so than in the later years of Henry VIII. If in the event the monasteries made the supreme sacrifice, many other interests in the realm, especially the secular clergy, had since 1531 been subjected to unprecedented grants and taxes. After Cromwell's time the bishops' lands were to be noticeably diminished by a series of one-sided deals with the Crown. Insofar as it seemed politic, even the laity were by no means neglected. Numerous gentle families were gouged by the system of wardships; profitable attainders crowded in from treasons, real or alleged; the ample Percy lands were assured to the King. Yet all these sources could not be made to yield a windfall of the size demanded for current problems and for endowment. For such a levy, where else could one turn than to the rich, defenceless, not very popular and—as it seemed to men like Cromwell—useless, decadent religious houses? The financial and political reasoning involved a simple process of *reductio ad absurdum* familiar to our own social-democratic minds. Englishmen have seldom proved slow to discover moral reasons for policies of material expediency, and the moral reason for regarding the political lightweight as the social irrelevance suggested themselves to Tudor minds as readily as to ours, and with even less conscious hypocrisy.

The general visitation of the monasteries began in July 1535 and lasted into the early months of the following year. Both by modern and even perhaps by contemporary standards of fairness, its conduct lies open to grave criticisms, and these, unlike so many others, may quite justifiably be levelled at Cromwell in person. He chose the visitors, supervised their work and was obviously concerned to produce a condemnatory document. On the other hand, enraged observers have too frequently applied the standards of modern royal commissions to a world where neither royal officials nor monks bore much resemblance to their present counterparts. A manuscript of the 86 articles of enquiry given to the visitors exists, with corrections in Cromwell's own hand. He no doubt also drew up the 25 injunctions to be given to the monks and nuns, though here he allowed additions at the discretion of the visitors themselves. These two documents have been denounced as a plan to make monastic life intolerable and to break the whole system by demanding impossible standards of loyalty and discipline. Yet apart from the injunction confining the religious to the precincts of their houses and forbidding them to receive visitors (one which, at least as a temporary measure, should not have worried those of genuine vocation), there is little or nothing in the injunctions which cannot be paralleled in those of innumerable episcopal visitations. While Cromwell can be credited with no serious scheme to reform monasticism, he cannot justly be charged with seeking to crush it by excessive disciplinary demands.

The visitors employed by him were all lawyers, either clerical or lay, with no admiration for the religious life. Dr. Richard Layton, Archdeacon of Buckingham and later Dean of York, was a garrulous cleric from whom the grosser tales mainly derive, but who nevertheless proved somewhat lax in imposing the injunctions upon the monks. His colleague Dr. Thomas Legh, a narrow-minded, legalist Cambridge don, would have none of this leniency and reported it to Cromwell, whereupon Layton countercharged Legh with arbitrary methods. With his 'satrapic countenance' and an arrogance of manner which offended his own cousin, the famous Bishop of Lichfield, Dr. Legh seems the least likeable of the visitors. He preserved, however, a certain reputation for impartiality and took trouble to obtain good pensions for certain prominent monks. A third visitor, Dr. John London, had in former times figured as a staunchly conservative Warden of New College, active in suppressing early Protestantism at Oxford. In later years he displayed equal zeal in enforcing the reactionary Six Articles. While he offended the Protestants by such actions, his disbelief in relics irritated old-fashioned opinion. Dr. London thus earned a bad press from both sides, and gave both a splendid theme for moralization by dying a few years later in the Fleet prison. Nevertheless, his letters to Cromwell show more signs of genuine concern for the expropriated religious than do those of his associates. One of his fellows at New College, Dr. Bedyll, also took part, as did Dr. John Tregonwell, another conservative in religion and destined to enjoy high favour in the days of Queen Mary. Dr. John ap Rice has been rightly described as 'a milder version of Dr. Legh', and should not be confused with his colleague Dr. Ellis Price, who operated only inside Wales and who, with that liberality of outlook which had long marked the Welsh clergy, took his mistress with him on progress. The houses of friars were visited separately by compliant members of their own orders like Richard Ingworth, suffragan Bishop of Dover, and Dr. Edward

Baskerville, yet another conservative, who under Elizabeth fell into trouble by refusing the Oath of Supremacy. In general, however, the unlucky fates alleged by Spelman to have befallen the buyers of monastic properties did not extend to Cromwell's monastic visitors, all of whom, except Dr. London, ended their lives in prosperity.

All these men must have been well aware that Cromwell expected their reports to give Parliament and public opinion an unfavourable picture of monastic life, and any visitors with moderately elastic consciences could easily satisfy this expectation. Without burdening their souls with gross fabrications and falsehoods, they could accept every accusation or piece of gossip. If tongues had wagged readily at any normal episcopal visitation, they could well be expected on this special occasion to wag with even greater malice. The monastic world was already disintegrating fast; morale was low, and every temptation existed for the less worthy to curry favour with the visitors. And even one or two monks with strong grudges could provide sufficient material for a damning report upon a house. Again, the too familiar mixing of monastic with lay society now had its nemesis. Unlike the bishops in the past, the Cromwellian visitors took notice of accusations from persons not members of the community concerned, and in the immediate neighbourhood there were always lay people who could be relied upon to supplement, accurately or inaccurately, the element of scandal. For visitors who had no wish to present a balanced picture, it was all too simple : one had merely to select the shade of grey which seemed acceptable. The haste with which these agents operated was admittedly often no greater than that displayed by many bishops in normal visitations, yet in neither case can a real sifting of alleged offences have been possible. The smaller monasteries of southern England having been visited by October 1535, Layton wrote to Cromwell that 'there is neither monastery, cell, priory, nor any other religious house in the north, but Dr. Legh and I have familiar acquaintance within ten or twelve miles of it, so that no knavery can be hid from us in the country'. They were consequently sent into the northern counties and perambulated them with such amazing expedition as to raise doubts whether they could even have been present at all the places claimed. Whatever their physical movements, they knew that Cromwell wanted the report by

February 1536, so that a dissolution-bill could be duly supported on the assembly of Parliament.

In passing judgement upon this cheap and nasty visitation, it seems reasonable to mention one or two slightly mitigating factors usually omitted amid the vociferous condemnations levelled against Cromwell and his hirelings. In matters of politics, justice, administration and religion, the age lacked that measure of balance and fair play which has more recently come to mark liberal western thought and behaviour. Just as controversialists, even naturally generous men like Thomas More, heaped un-measured contumely upon their opponents and could admit no ounce of good in them, so juries convicted unpopular defendants upon flimsy evidence, so litigants ascribed every subtle malice to their opponents, and so officialdom took the blackest possible view of individuals or of institutions it proposed to attack. If Legh and Layton were by our standards grossly unfair to monasteries, so were the bishops to Lutheran or Lollard groups. Again, the reports are not all unfavourable; Layton, for example, reported well on Durham, and Ap Rice upon Lacock. Likewise, in the very few cases where we can place a recent episcopal visitation alongside the *comperta* of the Cromwellian visitors, at least some of the latter's charges are shown to have been quite accurate. This is true of certain Yorkshire houses, where Archbishop Lee had recently exposed various of the offenders noted during their lightning tour by Legh and Layton. As already suggested, inde-pendent evidence shows that a number of houses deserved lurid reports, nor do these impressions rely solely upon episcopal en-quiries. A contemporary letter of the Abbot of Warden about ignorance, violence and vice amongst his own monks does not, for example, make pretty reading. Again, the many charges of homosexuality made (especially in the North) by Legh and Lay-ton may well be multiplied through malice, yet a number of such cases do occur in bishops' visitations and other respectable sources. That such offences sometimes arose in celibate but poorly-disciplined and ill-selected communities may surprise mid-twentieth century observers a trifle less violently than they used to surprise our Edwardian antiquaries. As for the supersti-tious relics preserved in monasteries, these were in fact very numerous, if on the whole very harmless. The women at Arden, for example, made offerings to the image of St. Bridget for their sick cows; others venerated the Virgin's milk at Clementhorpe or thought the girdle of St. Bernard at Newburgh helped those in labour. Such white magic was offensive to people who wanted a Christ-centred Christianity, yet it must have comforted many a poor creature and in many cases might well have been left to wither slowly in the sun.

The text of the Act of 1536, which dissolved religious houses with incomes under £200, displays some questionable features, notably the assumption that the line between 'vicious, carnal and abominable living' and adequate performance in religion could be drawn at this particular financial level. On the other hand, its provisions did no great violence to men and women of genuine vocation, and had it come twenty years earlier, it might have formed a prelude to genuine reform. The abbots and priors received very adequate pensions, especially in view of the fact that, on the average, they had only been presiding over miniature establishments of four or five persons. Some went to study at the university; some took benefices in addition to their pensions. As for the male rank and file, they were offered alternatives: either to receive 'capacities' allowing them to leave religion and serve as secular priests, or else to accept transfer to one of the greater houses of their respective orders. No complete statistics survive to indicate the proportion of those with weak vocations who took the former course. It was undoubtedly large. Of the 42 monks and canons in seven Sussex houses, no less than 38 took capacities. The Augustinian canons, the largest group in England, had even in normal times commonly served the parishes appropriated to their houses and so tended easily to assume the status of secular priests. On the other side, the majority of the Cistercians appear to have taken the opposite line: at Stanley all the monks desired to remain in religion, being transferred to Beaulieu and other Cistercian houses of the region. The prospect of transfer provided in itself a test of vocation.

As may be seen from their surnames, a large proportion of religious were drawn from the close vicinity of their houses; they might now be compelled to a radical change of background. With that small-mindedness characteristic of ingrowing academic or religious communities, the monks at the receiving house sometimes failed to make their guests welcome. When four Sawley monks arrived at Furness, the Abbot himself found excuses to repudiate them. Conversely, some of the newcomers refused to settle under new discipline: the former Abbot of Quarr chose to go to Beaulieu, but only to prove a quarrelsome member of this house. Yet in these respects we doubtless hear of the trying exceptions, not of the many who took the change in their stride. In making their choice, some shrewder monks and canons must have anticipated the ultimate fall of the greater houses, and have judged it wise to make their exit to a benefice before the flooding of the market by unemployed priests. Those of the rank-and-file who returned to the world at this first stage received gratuities, but no pensions: with these some expressed discontent, and the ill-fated Abbot of Barlings illegally sold the abbey plate to increase the rewards of his grumbling canons. When the final dissolution came, those who had stayed in religion were naturally pensioned along with their colleagues at the greater houses.

A feature of the interval between this first upheaval and the final act of 1539 was the sparing of numerous houses prepared to pay a heavy fine for the privilege. Of the 372 houses recorded by the *Valor* as having incomes under £200, only about 220 fell immediately. The whole Gilbertine order temporarily survived, thanks to the influence of its Master, Robert Holgate, a staunch Cromwellian, a future Lord President of the North and first Protestant Archbishop of York. Also during this interval, several prominent monks fell foul of the government and some, though by no means all, met the end of traitors. Adam Sedbergh, Abbot of Jervaulx, previously a supporter of the King, was precipitated into trouble by ex-Abbot Thirsk of Fountains, a bad ruler in his time of office and a busy intriguer in retirement. These two suffered execution, and Sedbergh's name, with the date 1537, may still be seen where he inscribed it in his prison in the Tower. Another semi-innocent victim was Abbot Paslew of Whalley, who pleaded guilty to a charge of treason, but had probably been implicated by ill-luck rather than by intention. Prior Wood of Bridlington, along with half-a-dozen other East Riding religious, was condemned on account of his part in Bigod's revolt. Mackerell of Barlings was an armed leader of the Lincolnshire Pilgrimage and paid the price. Through the attainder of their heads, the houses of Jervaulx, Whalley, Barlings, Bridlington and Kirkstead were deemed, by a dubious interpretation of the treason laws, to be dissolved.

Nevertheless, several of the prominent monks often assumed to have suffered with this group did in fact escape. One of these was Edward Kirkby, the former Abbot of Rievaulx, who spent six weeks in the Tower after the Pilgrimage and whose execution was rumoured. He is nevertheless known to have survived as a parish priest until 1557. The case of this man has recently been shown to contain none of the ingredients of martyrdom. Owing to violent internal quarrels at Rievaulx, its founder, the Earl of Rutland, had approached Cromwell to secure Kirkby's resignation. After protracted negotiations, he was induced to resign, and in 1534 received a handsome pension of £44 per annum. Kirkby then unsuccessfully tried to bribe Cromwell to reinstate him. When an Act of Parliament allowed his successor to halve the pension, Kirkby again engaged in prolonged efforts to get Cromwell's support and then tried to use the Pilgrimage of Grace to recover what he conceived his rights. Throughout the whole story, no political or religious principles were involved; Cromwell and numerous other people were put to enormous trouble because the Cistercian Order could not settle an internal quarrel. Another non-martyr was Lawrence Cooke, Prior of the Doncaster Carmelites, who, though specially excepted from the royal pardon and attainted, ended by receiving a pardon. Abbot Bolton of Sawley, though deeply implicated in the rebellion and condemned, may also belong to this group: there is no evidence that he was executed, and his name does not appear with the rest in the list of attainders for treason drawn up in 1540. Some other heads—Stonywell of Pershore, Love of Coggeshall and Peryn of Tavistock—were also accused of treasonable speeches, yet survived to enjoy their pensions.

Of these treason-actions brought against prominent monks, the most unjust were probably those of 1539 involving the three Benedictine abbots of Glastonbury, Reading and Colchester, who had all originally accepted the Royal Supremacy. Our knowledge of the charges brought against them remains imperfect, though the first two were regarded as implicated in the treason of the Poles and had supplied the northern rebels with money. In December 1539 Abbot Marshall of Colchester was reported by his servants and physician to have denounced the King's avarice, wished success to the Pilgrimage and asserted the unlawfulness of the dissolution of the greater monasteries. He denied to the last that he had ever asserted the Roman primacy. In the previous year, Abbot Hobbes of Woburn had been found by a local jury (including some staunch religious conservatives like John Gostwick) guilty of upholding the Pope's authority and condemning the royal divorce. Duly sentenced and executed, he may have stronger claims to be regarded as a Catholic martyr than the rest of this group. A few months later, Nicholas Heath, Prior of Lenton, also suffered for an attack on the King similar to that of Marshall.

In the examinations of some of these unfortunate suspects Cromwell was personally involved, and a note remaining in a list of his memoranda reads: 'The abbot of Reading to be sent down to be tried and executed at Reading with his complices, similarly the abbot of Glaston at Glaston'. Such a note truly represents one of the shadows upon Cromwell's reputation, yet M. Constant misunderstands its nature when he writes: 'Even before the trial, Cromwell had already, of his own authority, condemned the abbots to death.' Cromwell did not personally try these men, find them guilty and condemn them: he had no authority to do so. Therefore, if M. Constant's sentence means anything, it must mean that Cromwell suborned, bribed or threatened the juries at Reading and Glastonbury. But no evidence supports the suggestion, and this for a very good reason. In 1538–9 juries very readily convicted treason-suspects on flimsy evidence. Rebellions, plots, fear of foreign invasion, the burning and torture of English merchants in Spain, had produced their result: an exaggerated anxiety to appear ultra-loyal to an exacerbated monarch and an angry nation. Lord Russell, one of the more upright notables of the day, was among the commissioners who tried the Abbot of Glastonbury; however mistakenly, Russell thought the accused to have been justly condemned in a fair trial. The atmosphere was unhealthy and all too apt to produce harsh injustices, yet it was an atmosphere common to a large part of the nation and in no sense peculiar to the mind of the King's first minister. That overworked personage, compiling multitudinous memoranda for his private use, and knowing the facts of these cases, obviously assumed it a foregone conclusion that the abbots would be convicted of treason and executed. The spectacle remains unpleasant, and it is hard not to think of these cold phrases as throwing light upon the blunted, mechanical and calculating state of Cromwell's mind near the end of his career. Nevertheless, this is a vastly different matter from making him the sole author of judicial murders. Of this situation he was a victim as well as a partaker in a widely-shared responsibility. The national and international crisis had already developed when he took power: its embitterment cannot uniquely or even chiefly be blamed upon him or even upon the King. And if he could return to argue his case in retrospect, Cromwell would doubtless point out the fact that a major historical crisis was surmounted with little bloodshed precisely because, at the earliest sign of trouble, his government struck ruthlessly at the heart of the resistance. Weak and vacillating rulers, he would perhaps urge, ended by causing large-scale revolution, repression and slaughter. The abysses underlying this argument remain all too familiar from innumerable recent examples and the dilemma of power will remain as long as politics exists: it is the factor which must exclude men of sensibility from joining the unclean game in troubled times.

In 1536 Cromwell can scarcely have envisaged any immediate likelihood of a general dissolution of the greater monasteries, since the act of that year is allowed to describe the latter as 'divers and great solemn monasteries of this realm, wherein (thanks be to God) religion is right well kept and observed.' Nevertheless, the way was soon being smoothed for those greater houses prepared to make a voluntary surrender. The important abbey of Furness, which had narrowly avoided the treason-charges brought against its neighbour Whalley, took this line of least resistance early in 1537, and apparently with the genuine concurrence of the monks. In November the Cluniac priory of Lewes did likewise, closely followed by the Cistercians at Warden. Some heads were pressed into surrender by government agents; others hastened to London with seeming alacrity. Equally prominent during these years is an increase in the practice of collusive leases between religious houses and the local gentry. Even at the otherwise model house of Lacock, Abbess Temmes showered offices and long leases upon at least five of her male relatives, who continued to occupy a large part of the estates and to enjoy their various pensions long after the dissolution. A larger operator was Prior Munday of Bodmin, who issued very long leases to various of his kin and bribed his canons to permit the use of the convent seal for this purpose. It might further be added that Munday, formerly a canon of Merton, had recently been pushed into his office by the influence of his friends with Cromwell. Of the heads of the various houses at the surrender, a large number were Cromwell's recent appointees. They were safe men, prepared to accept the view that English monasticism was dead, to sur-

render without fuss when desired, to co-operate with the commissioners in an orderly and businesslike handover.

Between 1537 and 1540 surrenders were obtained from 158
male and 30 female houses. Meanwhile the orders of friars received separate treatment. They did not surrender house by house,
but within the year 1538 underwent a systematic suppression. In
this transaction Cromwell's chief agent was Richard Ingworth,
formerly Dominican prior of King's Langley and now suffragan
Bishop of Dover. His letters reflect to perfection that curious
combination of intimacy and subservience which marked the
attitude of so many subordinates towards Cromwell. The latter
stimulated his zeal by the reproach that, though he had changed
his habit, he had not yet changed his friar's heart. Ingworth vociferously replied, "Good, my lord, judge me not so, for God shall
be my judge, my friar's heart was gone two years before my
habit, saving only my living; but the favour [i.e. to the friars]
that I have showed hath not been for my friar's heart, but to
bring all things with the most quiet to pass'. He went on to
describe the brethren as mostly anxious to cast off their religion
and their habits, though as yet they lacked money to buy new
suits. Other prominent friars took a similar view. 'We all long
for a dispensation', wrote the Warden of the London Franciscans
to Cromwell, and he proceeded to elaborate the theory that God
has moved princes to take away their 'papistical and slanderous
apparel', just as he once corrected the children of Israel through
the Chaldeans and the Babylonians. The friars had become the
most deeply divided section of the regular clergy. Not only had
they developed a faction of extremist Protestants, but in many
places they had stirred up major local quarrels by their conten-
tious preaching against each other. Cromwell apparently regarded
them with impatience. Foxe, partially supported by the London
diarist Wriothesley, preserves an anecdote illustrating this attitude. Friar Gilbert Berkeley, a well-known Franciscan of Lincoln, Nottingham and York, became notorious for continuing to
wear his friar's cowl after the dissolution. Cromwell, walking
through St. Paul's churchyard, spied him in a shop. 'Yea', said
he, 'will not that cowl of yours be left off yet? And if I hear by
one o'clock that this apparel be not changed, thou shalt be
hanged immediately, for example to all others.' This harsh
warning Berkeley took to heart with great profit. He not only
put aside his cowl but accepted a living in Norfolk, married a

masterful wife, and ended as the henpecked Elizabethan Bishop of Bath and Wells.

The Dissolution Act of 1539 was primarily framed to grant full recognition to the long series of surrenders and to prevent any doubt about legal titles. It rehearses how many houses 'without constraint, coaction or compulsion of any manner of person or persons' had since 1536 surrendered to the King. It vests all their properties in the King, his heirs and successors, and then does likewise with those of all other monasteries 'which hereafter shall happen to be dissolved, suppressed, renounced, relinquished, forfeited, given up or by any other means come to his Highness'. One of this comprehensive list of fates had befallen every house by 23 March 1540, when last of all the Augustinian abbey of Waltham made its surrender. By this time Cromwell must have made Henry the richest ruler in Christendom, since for a brief space the King held nearly one-half of the wealth of the national Church which had voted him its Supreme Head.

Throughout these last months of Cromwell's career, the King and his ministers still maintained pious intentions to utilize a substantial proportion of the windfall in schemes for the rehabilitation of the Church. In particular, the insufficiency of bishops had already attracted their concern. As early as 1534 an Act of Parliament had named 26 towns for the sees of suffragan bishops, who could be appointed at the request of the appropriate diocesan. The offer was accepted in over half the possible cases during Cromwell's ministry, and it represents a useful extension of the former system, whereby suffragans with titles *in partibus infidelium* had been assisting the diocesan bishops. The dissolution of the monasteries now enabled the King to plan a much more important step: the creation and endowment of new dioceses. A manuscript in Henry's own hand sketches a plan for thirteen new sees based on monastic buildings and lands: for Essex at Waltham; for Buckinghamshire at Newnham; for Oxford, by joining Osney and Thame; for Nottingham, from Welbeck, Worksop and Thurgarton; for Cornwall, by uniting Launceston, Bodmin and some third house; for Lancashire and Richmondshire, by joining Fountains with the Archdeaconry of Richmond. The others proposed were Westminster, Peterborough, Gloucester, St. Albans, Dunstable, Leicester and Shrewsbury. Yet in the event, only six new bishoprics materialized: those of Peterborough, Gloucester, Oxford, Chester, Bristol and Westminster, the last-named only to be dissolved in 1550. The monastic chapters of Coventry, Rochester, Winchester, Ely, Durham, Carlisle and Norwich were abolished and replaced by deans and secular canons. To each a new code of statutes was presented, and together with the six entirely new sees, they henceforth became known as Cathedrals of the New Foundation. In addition, professorships of Greek, Hebrew, Theology, Law and Medicine were founded at Oxford and Cambridge. For this meagre settlement, with its tragically missed chances in the field of education and its curious disposition of sees, Cromwell cannot be blamed, since at the time of his fall the whole plan remained merely under discussion. The efficiency he displayed in other branches of Church-reform disposes one to think that he would have been dissatisfied with such piecemeal and lop-sided schemes.

Concerning monastic pensions, much is known from the voluminous records of the Court of Augmentations, the department which Cromwell erected to manage the new acquisitions of the Crown. Yet in the view of the present writer, the evidence is not quite satisfactorily set forth by Mr. Baskerville in his remarkable work *English Monks and the Dissolution of the Monasteries*. Here the abbots and priors, better documented than their inferiors, occupy too great a share of the picture. Nobody doubts their idyllic fate. Their pensions were liberal—often surprisingly so—and a fair proportion gravitated to bishoprics and other lucrative benefices. What, however, of the rank-and-file? it would seem that here the optimism of Mr. Baskerville has sometimes carried him a shade too far. The friars were turned out unpensioned, though it is true that many soon obtained clerical employment. When, for example, the Gloucester Dominicans were dissolved, they numbered a prior and six friars. Two years later, and again eight years later, espiscopal visitations were held : they show all the seven men serving as stipendiary priests in and around Gloucester, while at least two of these subsequently obtained actual benefices. Nuns were poorly pensioned, yet even so, like all incumbents and pensioners, had to pay their tenths to the King : I have before me, for example, a list of 1573 which shows several aged nuns paying tenths of 4s. on annual pensions of only £2 6s. 8d. The friars, whose houses had little or no property, and the nuns, who came mostly from poor houses, cannot by any stretch of imagination be regarded as handsomely provided for, and together these groups numbered at least three-eighths of the total body of ex-religious. The great majority of monks and canons received pensions in the close vicinity of five or six pounds per annum, which by the decade 1540–50 represents no more than the earnings of an unskilled labourer or the income of a very poor priest living on one chantry.

This situation—characteristically qualified by the fact that denizens of rich houses got larger pensions—suggests bare decency rather than generosity. Considerable numbers of male religious have been observed occupying benefices during the years succeeding the dissolution. To begin with, there were over 9,000 parishes, probably over 3,000 chantries, and an unknown number of private chaplaincies. Consequently a fair proportion of the 7,000 ex-religious priests may within a very few years have been absorbed as vacancies arose. Those unlucky during the first decade then presumably found things more difficult, since in 1549 the dissolution of the chantries threw a fresh group of priests upon the ecclesiastical labour-market, while greatly decreasing the number of emoluments available. Again, in 1552–3 the actual payment of pensions fell into serious arrears owing to the financial straits of Edward VI's government. Few monks and nuns traded their pensions, and the intrinsically improbable picture of astute pensioners outwitting innocent Augmentations officials (who were notoriously hardbitten) is disproved by the enquiries made at various times into the administration of pensions. Yet however many modifications should be imposed upon the optimism of Mr. Baskerville, there can be no return to the heroics of Gasquet or even to the more subdued lamentations of M. Constant. Mr. Baskerville was not entirely unfair or irrelevant when he implied that such people should first have studied the brutality with which both Catholic and liberal governments in Spain, France and Austria suppressed religious orders in the eighteenth and nineteenth centuries. The story of the dispossessed cannot be made into one of the great tragedies of English history. We should be even more misguided to shed many tears over the fate of monastic servants. The great majority, who worked out of doors, must have been readily employable by the new owners; at worst, they were in the position of other husbandmen of the time. Indoor servants, like the yeomen waiters and the barber at Butley Priory, would often have to seek employment elsewhere, but in some cases they are known to have been generously paid off with 'rewards' amounting to a year's wages. Both monastic stewards and corrodians were compensated or pensioned, and on every pension-list their names appear along with those of the monks and nuns. Altogether, we may safely scrap the old picture of an avalanche of sturdy beggars discharged from the closing gates of monasteries upon the highways of England; it is one of those many which may be relegated to the pages of the romancers and the propagandists.

Chapter Nine

Vicegerent in Spirituals

IN all seven editions of the Great Bible, an illustrated title-page illustrates Cromwell's pre-eminence as the direct intermediary between King and nation. Across the top of the page the King sits in state, delivering bibles with one hand to Cranmer and with the other to Cromwell. These recipients stand bare-headed, with expressions of great piety and accompanied by ecclesiastics and noblemen. Below this tableau the two dignitaries re-appear in a second scene; now wearing appropriate head-gear, they hand out bibles respectively to the clergy and the laity. At the bottom a large and picturesquely attired crowd of men and women are crying *Vivat Rex* and *God Save the King*. In the first three editions Cromwell's personal arms appear below his figure, but in the fourth and later ones, the effect is somewhat marred by the omission of these arms in favour of a blank space. These were the editions published after his fall and execution! Even though the plate was not, as often supposed, the work of Holbein, no doubt it seemed a pity to waste one so fine and so expensive.

Striking though it be, this picture tends to underestimate the functions of Cromwell as officially envisaged during his period of rule. In the field of ecclesiastical administration, as distinct from that of spiritual functions, the Archbishop was not in fact permitted a co-ordinate role with Cromwell. And in all matters affecting clerical discipline, The Vicegerent could and did issue orders directly to the clergy. The scope of his office was also vividly illustrated when Convocation opened on 16 June 1536, and Dr. William Petre not only appeared as Cromwell's deputy, but successfully asserted his own claim to take the chair, a tangible illustration of the Royal Supremacy which must have startled—and was presumably intended to startle—the bishops. On 21 June Cromwell attended in person to introduce the sen-

tence of nullity of marriage between the King and Anne
Boleyn, a document which both Houses obediently approved.
The great list of heresies known as the *mala dogmata* and presented to the Lower House on 23 June was not, as some writers
have supposed, an act of defiance against Cromwell or even
against his Lutheran allies. Practically every item it contains can be found in purely Lollard or Anabaptist cases of
heresy; the document constitutes a denunciation of popular extremism which was admittedly widespread, but which Cromwell
had taken no deliberate part in encouraging. On 11 July Cromwell attended Convocation once more in order to sign the Ten
Articles, the first of the Henrician formularies of the Faith.
These were presented by Edward Fox, Bishop of Hereford, one
of the prelates closest to Cromwell and who had recently been in
Germany negotiating with the Lutherans. On these grounds and
because they show some superficial similarities to the Wittenberg Articles, the Ten Articles have often been taken as mark-
ing a close *rapprochement* between the government and the
Lutherans; but on closer examination, as M. Constant and others
have made clear, the resemblance largely vanishes. Though the
Ten Articles adopt Melancthon's formulae on questions not in
dispute with the Catholics, their divergence from Lutheran doctrine is in many places obvious. They do not, as often supposed,
reduce the seven sacraments to three: they merely define the
sacraments of baptism, penance and the eucharist without giving any total number. On penance, they contradict the Lutherans
by retaining auricular confession and by asserting that penance
is a sacrament of divine institution and necessary for salvation.
On ceremonies they do similarly, by praising the veneration of
images and virtually the whole range of Catholic observances.
They also retain prayers for the dead. Needless to stress, their
eucharistic position remains staunchly orthodox. Altogether,
they were clearly dominated by the personal outlook of the King,
who, even when Cromwell most desired to encourage the
Lutheran princes, would make no more than a series of minor
diplomatic gestures. The ugly consequences for Cromwell of this
insular, self-confident and conservative attitude will soon become
apparent.

A most interesting illustration of his official relationship with
the bishops derives from the tract *Of the Authority of the Word
of God against the Bishop of London*, published about 1540 by

the Scottish Reformer Alexander Alesius, whom Cromwell and Cranmer had called from exile in Antwerp and who, rebuffed by theological conservatives in Cambridge, had come to study and practise medicine in London. Alesius describes in detail a debate held early in 1537 by Cromwell and the bishops concerning the number of the sacraments. This meeting he places 'in the Parliament House', and though Foxe, who borrows his account almost verbatim, arbitrarily alters this to 'the Convocation House', it was not a formal meeting of the Upper House of Convocation. However prejudiced, Alesius is a first-hand authority, since Cromwell happened to encounter him in the street and took him along to the conference. On their arrival, the Scotsman noticed that the bishops did obeisance to Cromwell and that he sat in the highest place. Opening the proceedings, he thanked his hearers on behalf of the King for their assembly to determine the controversies surrounding the Christian religion. The King, he continued, studied night and day 'to set a quietness in the church'. His desire was 'to set a stay for the unlearned people, whose consciences are in doubt what they may believe'. Although the King 'by his excellent learning knoweth these controversies well enough', he will allow no alterations save by consent of Convocation and his whole Parliament. He desired them to set aside malice and obstinacy, to debate 'friendly and lovingly', without brawling and scolding. The King would not suffer Scripture to be defaced with glosses and papistical laws, or by the mere authority of doctors and Councils of the Church. Much less would he admit doctrines not contained in Scripture but approved only by continuance of time and old custom, and by unwritten verities, 'as ye were wont to do'. His Majesty would give them high thanks if they could attain a godly and perfect unity, 'whereunto this is the only way and mean, if ye will determine all things by the Scripture, as God commandeth you in Deuteronomy; which thing His Majesty exhorteth and desireth you to do'.

Our observer Alesius then provides a long, interesting, but doubtless unfair and self-centred account of the debate which ensued. The Catholic view of the sacraments was most earnestly defended by Stokesley, Bishop of London, whom Cromwell reproved by name for defending mere 'unwritten verities'. After a speech by Cranmer, Cromwell turned to Alesius and commanded him to declare his opinion, introducing him to the bishops as 'the King's scholar' and desiring them to hear him impartially. Alesius, no doubt elated by this chance opportunity, cited the Scriptures and St. Augustine to prove that only two sacraments, Baptism and the Lord's Supper, could claim divine institution. Edward Fox, just back from Germany, gave him general support. Thanks to the diligence of the Germans, said the Bishop of Hereford, the gospel was now shining before the world, and Truth the daughter of Time would triumph. So encouraged, Alesius made another plea that the sacraments should be limited to those two instituted by Christ.

In his reply Bishop Stokesley continued to maintain the authority of the Councils and old doctors of the church, to the polite amusement of the enlightened. 'Now when the right noble Lord Cromwell, the Archbishop, with other bishops who did defend the pure doctrine of the gospel, heard this, they smiled a little one upon another, forasmuch as they saw him flee, even in the very beginning of the disputation unto his old rusty sophistry and unwritten verities.' Alesius would then have proceeded further to confute what Foxe calls 'this blasphemous lie', but the Vicegerent bade him to be content, 'for the time began to go away, and it was twelve o'clock'. On the next day, Alesius again attended Cromwell, but a message from Cranmer warned them of the hostility of the conservative bishops and caused Cromwell to keep his champion from harm by excluding him from the debate. Instead, he bade Alesius give him his notes to show the bishops at some future opportunity. 'Thus', concludes Foxe, 'through the industry of Cromwell, the colloquies were brought to this end, that albeit religion could not wholly be reformed, yet at that time there was some reformation had throughout all England.'

This account of the conference provides, despite its partisan character, a valuable glimpse of Cromwell's official role as moderator in the great controversy. He is first of all deputy and spokesman for a king with strong theological views, yet he is also the well-informed layman capable of understanding the tenor of the disputations. He does not personally bandy the texts and the dogmas, yet he is no merely neutral chairman. While avoiding any suspicion of sacramentarian heresy, he distinctly backs the advanced party and brings to the conference a theologian of foreign background, one who stood as far to the left as any man could safely stand in Henrician England. Moreover he introduces this controversial outsider as one enjoying royal patronage, and deliberately uses him to confound the conservative bishops, a far stronger element on the bench than the account of Alesius would suggest. As might be expected from his championship of the vernacular Bible, Cromwell strongly supported those who wanted a doctrinal settlement based closely upon the Scriptures and excluding the unwritten traditions, medieval doctors and General Councils of the Church. That some measure of social and even religious idealism was probably involved in this attitude, we have already suggested. Yet Cromwell was no doubt also astute enough to realize the very considerable flexibility of action allowed by the Bible to princes and governors, astute enough to foresee that if a quietness should be successfully imposed upon warring consciences and factions, it would owe more to politic power than to the intrinsic simplicities of holy writ.

In the August of 1536 Cromwell had issued to the clergy his first set of injunctions, a characteristic and mundane programme of decent, practical reforms. It is a fundamentally secular document, not closely modelled upon episcopal injunctions, yet constructive and enlightened in its social and educational emphases. The clergy are ordered to instil into the young, both by admonition to parents and by direct teaching, their *pater noster*, articles of the faith and ten commandments in the mother tongue. In their sermons they must teach these clause by clause, till the whole be known. They must urge upon parents the need to place their children to learning, or to some honest occupation or husbandry, lest the young fall into begging and stealing. Daily we see valiant men descending into these courses, says Cromwell, because their parents suffered them to be nurtured in idleness, whereas, 'if they had been well educated and brought up in some good literature, occupation or mystery, they should, being rulers of their own family, have profited as well themselves as divers other persons, to the great commodity and ornament of the common weal'. Rich clergymen, he continues, shall give exhibitions to scholars at Oxford, Cambridge, or in some grammar school, one for every hundred pounds of annual income. A miscellany of precepts follows. The people must not be allured into superstitious devotions to images and relics; the clergy must avoid card-playing and alehouses. All non-resident incumbents with £20 a year or more are ordered to distribute before the churchwardens a fortieth part of their incomes to the poor inhabitants. Incumbents must also be prepared to bestow the fifth part of their benefices towards the repairs of chancels, when these are their legal responsibility.

If few ecclesiastical historians have praised these injunctions, this is presumably because of their source. But they represent precisely what any sensible, educated, middle-class layman had to say to the mid-Tudor English Church. Few forward-looking churchmen can have quarrelled with such principles, even though the Church itself was powerless to enforce them. It is perhaps the uneasy feeling that Cromwell was the only authority capable of imposing simple and obvious reforms upon the Church which has earned him so much hostility from ecclesiasts. They have always found it easier to harp on the fact that Cromwell destroyed the monasteries than to recall that he strove to make the clergy perform a more positive and humane function in society, one which they have in fact come to exercise.

The work was continued by a second set of injunctions dated September 1538, the most important provision of which has already been described. Yet this placing of bibles in the churches, planned in 1536 but now enforced, should also be seen within the context of the educational proposals which distinguish both sets of injunctions. By those of 1538 the clergy are bound not merely to set up bibles and refrain from discouraging readers, but even 'expressly provoke, stir and exhort every person to read the same, as that which is the very lively word of God, that every Christian person is bound to embrace, believe and follow if they look to be saved, admonishing them nevertheless to avoid all contention and altercation therein, but to use an honest sobriety in the inquisition of the true sense of the same, and to refer the explication of obscure places to men of higher judgement in scripture'. Every Sunday and holy day the clergy are required to recite to their parishioners twice, thrice or oftener if need be, a sentence of the *pater noster* or creed in English, so that all may learn them by heart. These essentials once learned, the parishioners may then be taught to understand them. Parents and householders must be exhorted to pass on this teaching to their children and servants. Likewise the people must be taught the ten commandments by heart. At confessions every Lent, the clergy must examine every person as to whether he can recite the articles of their faith and the *pater noster* in English. Those who are not perfect should be told that every Christian person should know these things before receiving the blessed sacrament; they may even be threatened with possible future injunctions debarring the ignorant from communion. Sermons must be provided by incumbents at least quarterly; these shall purely and sincerely declare the gospel of Christ and exhort the hearers to works of charity, mercy and faith—especially those prescribed by Scripture—and to avoid reposing their trust in works devised by men's unscriptural fantasy, as in wandering on pilgrimages, offering money, candles or tapers to images and relics, 'kissing or licking the same', or saying over a number of beads 'not understanded nor minded on'. Images thus abused must be removed; no candles, tapers or waxen figures must be set before any image or picture; parishioners must be admonished that 'images serve for no other purpose but as to be books of unlearned men, that can no letters'. Non-resident parsons must appoint curates able to execute these injunctions and stand responsible for any default. Incumbents shall admit no unlicensed preachers, yet they shall offer no resistance to those who are duly licensed by the King, the archbishop or the bishop of the diocese.

More firmly than any of their contemporaries, Cromwell and his party had grasped the point that it was upon instruction in the elements of the faith, rather than upon ecclesiastical courts and legal coercion, that the future position of the Church in society must depend. This conviction was by no means the prerogative of Englishmen or of Protestants; in these same years the Jesuits were working their way to the same basic conclusions.

On a less exalted level, but also in accordance with these injunctions, Cromwell's agents proceeded in 1538 to a general assault upon images and saints' shrines to which pilgrimage was made. Especially prominent among these agents was the former Dominican Dr. John Hilsey, who had succeeded Fisher in the see of Rochester, and who exposed the Blood of Hales, the Rood of Boxley and other time-honoured frauds. His early death in the same year removed one of the ablest minds in the Cromwellian group. To this episode there are obviously two sides. The destruction of important works of art and the predatory confiscation of the rich treasures at the shrines of Winchester, Chichester and Canterbury have been quite justifiably deplored. On the other side, there can be no question but that gross superstition and even fraudulent rascality surrounded some of these places: later generations, in which light-headed materialism of this type no longer forms a burning issue, have all too easily invested it with picturesque romanticism. There occurred in the middle thirties a very real revulsion against these abuses. Its coarse, plebeian side can be seen in the ballad *The Fantasy of Idolatry*, printed by Foxe. A more educated and naïvely idealist aspect can be seen in *The Fall and Evil Success of Rebellion*, written in 1537 by the Yorkshire gentleman Wilfrid Holme, who exultantly sees the New Learning sweeping away the cobwebs of monkery, magic, idolatry, ungodly pseudo-science and the hair-splitting metaphysics of the schoolmen, while the nation marches forward to a glorious future, led by a devout monarch and guided by a Christocentric religion based on the Gospels. In short, the story belongs to the Erasmian Renaissance as well as to the English Reformation. The most spectacular victim of this eikonoclasm, the shrine of Becket at Canterbury, had also important political connotations; in reply to the papal threats which followed its destruction, the King issued a manifesto denouncing Becket as a 'rebel who fled into the realm of France and to the Bishop of Rome to procure the abrogation of wholesome laws'. Cromwell stood amongst the prime movers as well as the executors of this campaign. Foxe states that the 'fresh and quick wits pertaining to his family' were responsible for 'divers excellent both ballads and books . . . concerning the suppression of the Pope and all popish idolatry'. Foxe's tastes were admittedly not ours, but the evidence was badly abused by the eminent Victorian clericals who used this passage to make Cromwell 'the great patron of ribaldry, and the protector of the ribalds, of the low jesters, the filthy ballad-mongers, the ale-house singers . . . in short, of all the blasphemous mocking and scoffing which disgraced the Protestant party'. The one example cited by Foxe was not written by a member of Cromwell's household, nor was ballad-writing limited to the Protestant faction.

From our examination of the injunctions of 1538 we have omitted the best known, which reads as follows: 'Item that you and every parson, vicar or curate . . . shall for every church keep one book or register wherein ye shall write the day and year of every wedding, christening and burying made within your parish for your time, and so every man succeeding you likewise.' To provide for the safe keeping of the register, the parish shall provide 'one sure coffer with two locks and keys', the one to remain with the incumbent, the other with the churchwardens.

Every Sunday the book must be duly entered up in the presence of at least one of the wardens. For every omission the guilty party shall forfeit 3s. 4d. to the church repair fund. Even this valuable innovation was greeted by Victorian ecclesiastical backbiting. Canon Dixon, who calls it 'but an inadequate attempt to supply the loss of the registers of various kinds which had been kept by the monks', should have known better. No medieval monk ever kept anything remotely resembling a parish register : the occasional note in a monastic register concerning the death of some notability or some aristocratic patron of the house does not give it even a distant family resemblance to the record under discussion. Cardinal Ximenes is said first to have introduced parish registers in his province of Toledo in 1497; they were ordered in France the year after Cromwell began them in England, but they became general throughout Catholic countries only after the Council of Trent. It is possible, but unproven, that Cromwell may have encountered such records during his travels on the Continent. There can certainly be no question regarding the necessity of the reform. To the laity parish registers were infinitely more useful than they are today. No parallel records then existed, and in the small communities of the period, marriages within the prohibited degrees were all too likely to occur. Conversely, divorces disguised as decrees of nullity were often sought not merely on grounds of blood-relationship, but on the absurd ground of spiritual affinity contracted between a baptised person and his kin on the one hand, and his sponsors and their kin on the other. A case is cited in England where a man was punished for incest because he had married as his second wife the goddaughter of his first. A hierarchy which could evolve these legal fantasies and yet fail to organize any systematic records of marriages, baptisms and deaths was indeed inviting forcible reform at the hands of the State. The need was obvious enough to a number of humble parish clergymen in various parts of early sixteenth-century England. If we wish to observe the pre-history of parish registers, we must make a mighty effort, dismiss monks from our minds, and look at the few surviving parish registers kept before the date of Cromwell's order. At Tipton in Staffordshire a register was maintained, if somewhat scrappily, from 1513. Altham, Lancashire, has one with many entries ranging from 1518 to 1533, while at Perlethorpe and Carburton, both in Nottinghamshire, there are entries as early as 1528. Some dozen· others beginning between 1530 and 1538 are still in existence. No doubt all these represent the efforts of a small minority of exceptionally conscientious priests, yet there must have been more of these primeval registers which have since perished: at this period there existed among the parish clergy a good deal of spontaneous commonsense waiting to be organized.

At the same time, suspicious people in the remoter provinces assumed, apparently without the slightest grounds, that the plan contained a trap; that Cromwell entertained unpleasant fiscal motives. As early as 1536 rumours of such intentions were already current among the northern rebels. Among the many false reports which contributed to the Pilgrimage of Grace, there came the rumour that christenings, marriages and burials would now be taxed. In 1538 again, Sir Piers Edgecombe reported to Cromwell that in Devon and Cornwall the people feared lest the King and his Council should cause parsons to 'make a book wherein is to be specified the names of as many as be wedded and buried and christened. Their mistrust is, that some charges more than hath been in times past shall grow to them by this occasion of registering.' Despite these prejudices, the decree speedily took effect. At first the registers were kept in paper books, or even on loose sheets, but in 1598 incumbents received orders to have their early registers transcribed into parchment books. Not all did so, but of the 800 surviving registers which date back to 1538–9, the great majority are preserved in the form of these later copies: only in a few cases have the paper originals survived. Today, when our early parochial archives have merely historical and genealogical interest, we need a new Cromwell to ensure their safe keeping, perhaps in regional repositaries where they could be cared for and readily consulted by scholars. Meanwhile, a still superb if somewhat depleted treasury of parochial records should occasionally remind us of Cromwell's contribution to the cause of order and efficiency in Church and State.

The protection extended by Cromwell to Protestant heretics does not depend on the several anecdotes retailed by Foxe: it appears in the Act of Attainder and could easily be deduced from several of the state-papers. It therefore comes as a surprise to be told by at least two well-known historians that the heretic John Lambert 'was condemned to death by Cromwell'. How much truth lies in this statement can easily be verified by anyone who troubles to read the only source of importance: Foxe's vivid narrative of this *cause célèbre*. Lambert, a former Fellow of Queen's College, Cambridge, and chaplain to the Merchant Adventurers at Antwerp, had been in trouble for heresy on many occasions, not only with More and Warham in earlier years, but recently before the Reforming bishops, Cranmer, Shaxton and Latimer. Even Robert Barnes, terrified lest the Lutherans should be tarred with the brush of extremism, joined in reporting it to authority when Lambert took the extremist Zwinglian line on the eucharist. Undeterred, Lambert also denied the right of bishops to jurisdiction, and then made the mistake of appealing from them to the King. His appeal came at a moment when Henry was seeking not only to placate conservative English opinion, but also to achieve agreement with one or both of the great Catholic powers. He therefore saw in Lambert's case a splendid opportunity to demonstrate the orthodoxy and majesty of caesaro-papalism in England, and on 16 November 1538, he staged a magnificent heresy-trial at Whitehall. Arrayed in pure white to symbolize high ecclesiastical jurisdiction, and surrounded by his bishops and peers, Henry personally subjected the unfortunate Lambert to one of the most terrifying judicial ordeals of history. The vulgar and easy process of browbeating to which the Supreme Head descended has too often been described to warrant full repetition. Having brushed aside Lambert's nervous qualifications, Henry caused him to deny the Real presence and then retorted, 'Mark well, for now thou shalt be condemned by Christ's own words, *Hoc est corpus meum*'. After this brilliant dialectical triumph, he gave Lambert five hours of disputation with successive bishops in the face of a hostile, noisy audience. At first the victim put up a gallant performance, but in the last stages he relapsed into a daze, broken by a few spasmodic interjections. Torches were brought, and when the last bishop had finished, the King asked Lambert whether he would live or die. 'My soul I commend to God', replied the exhausted heretic, 'my body I submit to your clemency'. But Henry's patience was also exhausted : 'If you do submit yourself unto my judgement, you must die, for I will be no patron of heretics. Cromwell, read the sentence of condemnation against him.' The Vicegerent, who had not yet opened his mouth, obeyed. How could he do otherwise? Only in this nominal sense did Cromwell condemn Lambert to death.

Protestant opinion held that Gardiner had engineered the

whole affair, so as to put Cromwell in a dilemma: either he must openly read the sentence against a heretic or be suspected by the King of heresy. In some degree this was Cromwell's situation, but the intrigue attributed to Gardiner may well be a hostile fabrication, whereby later Protestants like Foxe tried to cover their embarrassment. By blaming the *bête noire* of Winchester, one withdrew attention from the spectacle of Barnes and other Lutherans helping to get a sacramentarian heretic into trouble. If Cranmer and Cromwell felt hostile eyes directed upon themselves, they do not seem to have behaved with conspicuous nervousness. At the trial Cranmer dealt charitably with 'brother Lambert'. As for Cromwell, he sent for the condemned man on the morning of his execution and held a secret interview with him in his private room, after which Lambert breakfasted with the gentlemen in Cromwell's hall. When Foxe wrote, these were verifiable facts which he is unlikely to have invented. When, however, he continues, 'it is reported of many that Cromwell desired [Lambert] of forgiveness for that he had done', he was merely repeating the rumour which would naturally arise after a secret interview and an especially revolting execution. On the other side, those who have cited one of Cromwell's official letters as representing his real view of the trial have offended against the probabilities. In writing to Sir Thomas Wyatt in Paris, Cromwell lauded the King's excellent gravity, the inestimable majesty with which he exercised the office of Supreme Head, the benignity with which he essayed to convert the miserable man. 'I wished the princes and potentates of Christendom to have had a mete place for them there to have seen it. Undoubtedly they should have much marvelled at his Majesty's most high wisdom and judgement, and reputed him none otherwise after the same than in manner the mirror and light of all other kings and princes in Christendom.' This passage need not and probably does not represent Cromwell's own thoughts, nor does it throw doubt upon Foxe's less edifying account of the King's performance. The French court was one of the chief targets of Lambert's propaganda-trial, while here was the lesson which Henry expected Cromwell to disseminate in Paris and throughout Europe. And when it came to such flatteries, even the trowel advocated by Disraeli was no adequate implement for the needs of Henry VIII.

Chapter Ten

Foreign Policy and the Reaction

FROM the moment of England's rupture with the Papacy in 1533, foreign relations exerted little effect upon the internal Reformation. They nevertheless form one substantial strand of the rope which dragged Cromwell to disaster, and we cannot end the story without a glance in their direction. In his speech of 1523 Cromwell had already shown himself the holder of hard-headed views on English foreign policy. It seems likely enough that he shared the anti-French prejudices of his generation, yet he had fully emancipated himself from the romantic Agincourt-mentality which survived at every level of English society into the reign of Henry VIII. He had not, however, enjoyed the training which makes a great foreign minister. While his earlier career had helped him to a consummate grasp of the economic aspects of international relations, Wolsey had not given him diplomatic experience, and from his rise to power he became so deeply immersed in administrative reform, ecclesiastical policy and the overwhelming detail of current administration that he can scarcely have perfected his knowledge, or devoted much basic thinking to foreign affairs. More important, he never held un-disputed control of the field.

On Wolsey's fall Henry had personally assumed the super-vision of external relations, and during the period 1532–40 we seldom or never witness a truly Cromwellian negotiation. The King's trenchant if spasmodic intelligence had brought him to a viewpoint which events were destined in large part to justify. The costly and disappointing entanglements into which Wolsey had led the nation disposed Henry to seek a position of friendly neutrality between the two great Continental rivals, Francis I and Charles V, and to avoid alliances which might involve war. It must be admitted that during the early thirties he did not show conspicuous ability in his efforts to attain this ideal.

Though at first he needed the help of Francis towards the obtaining of his divorce at the hands of the Pope, he needlessly alienated that King in 1533 by his rudeness in sending an independent embassy to Pope Clement while the latter was the guest of Francis upon French soil. There are no strong reasons for accepting the supposition that this insult sprang from the advice of Cromwell, though it seems certain that the latter, his eye on the supreme economic importance of the Netherlands, was already leaning towards an understanding with their ruler Charles V. Doubtless he was also completely sceptical concerning these last-minute hopes of wringing a divorce from the Pope. So long, however, as Katherine of Aragon lived and her nephew Charles retained a sense of family duty, any *modus vivendi* between England and Charles proved too difficult to achieve; moreover, during the years between the divorce and Katherine's death. Henry showed a lack of decency in his shabby treatment of Katherine and her daughter, treatment duly reported by Chapuys to Charles and the reverse of conciliatory in its effects. Having thus lacerated both great powers, Henry did not scruple to rub salt in the wounds by such actions as the execution of Fisher and More, which, unlike the burning of obscure Anabaptists or the hanging of humble rebels, had an immense notoriety-value throughout the courts of Europe. Assuming that Henry's broad objective was sensible, nothing can appear less effective than his methods during these years, and the contrast so strongly implied by Merriman between the all-wise Henry and the blundering Cromwell would seem by no means applicable to the facts of the case. Indeed, the consistency with which Henry desired a policy of detachment may always be questioned, the more so because after Cromwell's death he himself departed from it so disastrously as to furnish the supreme example of its wisdom.

Under the circumstances obtaining in the early years of his ministry, Cromwell's cautious mind inevitably turned towards the notion of discovering allies, and as he surveyed the European scene, few potentially useful suggestions presented themselves. But one new constellation was in the ascendant and—for all an observer could tell at this moment—might soon dominate the heavens. The Lutheran princes of Germany, led by the Elector of Saxony and the Landgrave of Hesse, had in 1530–31 banded together in self-defence against the Emperor and formed the League of Schmalkalde. While the future extension of Lutheranism could not be predicted, it was obvious both to France and to England that the multifarious difficulties of Charles would most likely prevent him from crushing these princes, whose military and diplomatic weight might, in a world so delicately balanced, be manipulated with decisive effect. It is certain that Cromwell had already decided to explore this field by the summer of 1533, when his close friend Stephen Vaughan was one of two agents sent to tour Germany and report on the state of politics and religion in that troubled country. And from the first it was obvious that an ideological banner could be flaunted to attract the Lutherans. In January 1534 Nicholas Heath and Christopher Mont were despatched to tell them that the King of England had also become an enemy to the Pope and would willingly join with them to extirpate false doctrine. Their response proved frigid, for the princes were not fools; they took religion with deadly seriousness and perhaps already suspected the authenticity of Henry's Protestantism.

While nothing arose for the moment from this first overture, another interesting Protestant connection soon came under review. Under the guidance of violent Reformers led by the demagogue Georg Wullenwever, the great Hanseatic city of Lübeck was seeking to dispose of the vacant throne of its neighbour and rival Denmark. These Lübeckers were people genuinely in need of English help, and they had the means to flatter Henry's egotism. In August 1534 he signed a treaty with the city whereby, in return for an English loan of 50,000 gulden, Lübeck promised to support his divorce and denial of Roman authority, and also (should he decide to accept) help him to the throne of Denmark. Visions of Scandinavian hegemony floated before Henry's eyes, and the plan at least offered a means to deflate the pretensions of the Emperor, since the latter had proposed his own candidate for the Danish crown. By the signing of the treaty, however, the enterprise had already begun to go astray. The mercurial Wullenwever had also approached the nearby Duke of Holstein with an offer of the crown. On his refusal, the Lübeckers had angrily invaded Holstein, but had been shocked to find themselves driven back and their city besieged. At this stage the Danes had themselves taken a hand by offering their throne to the Duke, who had thus in July 1534 become Christian III. This event destroyed the contention of Lübeck that it desired to introduce pure religion into Denmark, since the new King was himself a Rutheran. At this time, Robert Barnes, the former friar and Lutheran missionary, had embarked upon a fresh phase of his stormy career by crossing to Hamburg and acting as an official emissary to the Lutheran states. In the summer of 1534 Barnes was advising the King to extricate himself from the Lübeck alliance and to ally with King Christian. As yet, Henry's pride forbade this rational course, and he gave ships and two skilled engineers to assist the Lübeckers. When Christian sent over an embassy to demand an explanation, Cromwell was assigned the task of bluffing and lying, though he had assisted in these negotiations only in a subordinate capacity. After further victories by Christian and the loss of some English ships, Wullenwever fell from power and suffered execution; hence the summer of 1535 saw Henry's withdrawal from the unlucky and ill-judged scheme. Its cost admittedly did not begin to compare with that of a campaign in France, yet Henry had succeeded in alienating the very power which he desired to attract: that of Lutheran princes, to several of whom Christian was related. Only in February 1536 was England able to make a treaty with Denmark which mitigated this unfortunate situation.

Meanwhile in 1534-5 French relations at first promised to improve, but then deteriorated still further. King Francis took the initiative by sending two embassies to arrange dynastic marriages: first that of the Princess Mary, then that of her baby step-sister Elizabeth, to a French prince. It was on the former of these occasions that the ambassador Admiral de Brion tried to frighten Cromwell by the suggestion of an alliance between Charles and Francis, directed against England. Cromwell had done his best to cater for French tastes by sending for beautiful young ladies to come to court and entertain the visitors. Finally he appeared with a parting gift for de Brion, but the latter approached Chapuys with ostentatious civility and declared that if they two could only bring their masters to accord, all would go well. Henry and Cromwell doubtless understood the element of bluff in such a demonstration, but from about this time a Catholic alliance against heretical England loomed amongst the more fearsome possibilities. The threat might also present opportunities to either power if it wished to cajole or blackmail England into helping it against the other. In 1535 Francis, encouraged by the temporary absence of Charles in Tunis, brusquely demanded financial support from England to help him attack Milan; he then seized English ships at Bordeaux, causing Cromwell and Gardiner to make repeated efforts to obtain their release.

With both great powers thus unfriendly, if not as yet united against England, it now seemed appropriate to bid once more for the support of the Lutheran princes, whose influence and beliefs were rapidly gaining ground throughout the German states. After Barnes had exercised some preliminary blandishments, Edward Fox, Bishop of Hereford, went on an embassy late in the year and obtained a conditional offer from the Lutherans to recognize Henry VIII as Defender and Protector of their League. Their condition was a hard one for Henry: he must first accept the Confession of Augsburg, make it a basis for the Reformation in England and defend it at any future General Council of the Church. His reply showed the firmness of his intention never to become a Lutheran or to import a religion made in Germany. He answered that he had long been minded to set forth true doctrine, but being a King reckoned somewhat learned (a conscious understatement), and having learned men in his kingdom, he could not accept from anyone the faith of the realm, which was grounded in the Scriptures. His attitude towards the Lutherans showed no significant variations. He saw no harm in allowing Barnes, Fox and Heath to argue theology at Wittenberg, so long as he remained uncommitted and very much master in his own house.

At this moment, in January 1536, when both France and the Germans seemed broken reeds, Queen Katherine died and thus opened the way for a new *rapprochement* with the Emperor. The very next day Cromwell instructed Gardiner to assure the French Government that this event had removed 'the only matter of unkindness' between Henry and Charles, and to remain 'the more aloof and be the more "froyt" and cold in relenting' to any French overtures or requests. He felt that the blackmail-weapon had now changed hands. Francis took the hint and began efforts to regain Henry's support. Meanwhile Cromwell also saw Chapuys, urging upon him that no reason now remained for hostility. The Emperor was nothing if not hardheaded; his relations with France were still strained and formed but one of the many problems which beset his vast Empire. Thus it was not long before Henry enjoyed the delicious spectacle of both great powers bidding for his support. At this stage, however, Cromwell seems for the first time to have pressed a policy of his own, for he went to Henry along with Chapuys to propose an Anglo-Imperial alliance. The request again makes one wonder whether Henry had hitherto been very decisive about his policy of disengagement: certainly he cannot have explained such purposes with clarity to his chief minister.

At all events, his mind was now resolved and, according to Chapuys, a piquant scene ensued in the Privy Chamber. After the Imperial Ambassador had offered terms for negotiation, the King took Cromwell and Audley out of earshot and seemed to be angrily disputing with the former. 'After a considerable time, Cromwell grumbling left the conference in the window where the King was, excusing himself that he was so very thirsty that he was quite exhausted—as he really was with pure vexation—and sat down on a coffer out of sight of the King, where he sent for something to drink.' Henry then came across to Chapuys and closed the interview with various rude remarks against the Emperor. Later that day Chapuys called on Cromwell, whom he found so upset 'that he was hardly able to speak for sorrow, and had never been more mortified in his life than with the said reply'. We do not know the precise proposals and arguments used during this altercation between Henry and Cromwell; it is extremely improbable that the latter could have favoured an offensive alliance likely to involve large-scale Continental warfare. Nevertheless, Henry appears justified in his refusal of any Imperial alliance, since extensive hostilities between Francis and Charles soon broke out again and continued throughout most of the years 1536-7. During this period—the cleverest phase of Henry's foreign policy—the King pretended he would gladly arbitrate 'for the peace and weal of Christendom', while in actual fact seeking to embroil the contestants still further. In accordance with such a directive, Cromwell ordered our ambassadors at both courts to give 'an answer so general that it doth neither refuse their alliance, nor much encourage them to conceive that they may without difficulty obtain their desire'.

This fortunate conjuncture of foreign affairs left the government unimpeded to crush the Pilgrimage of Grace, but by the autumn of 1537 the exhausted contestants on the Continent arrived at a truce, one destined soon to strengthen in a manner sinister to the interest of England. The subsequent year saw Henry, once more without a wife and engaged in collecting portraits of the Duchess of Milan and other noble dames, with a view to strengthening his position by a foreign marriage-alliance. He even suggested through his agent at the French court that a number of possibles should be brought to Calais to undergo his personal inspection, and altogether made himself so ridiculous as to invite a taunt from the French ambassador Castillon which drew a blush even to his own cheek. Making no progress in this enterprise, he then transparently sought to embroil the Emperor and France by dangling the prospect of marriage alliances between his daughter Mary and princes of both these powers. While such overtures were in progress, Cromwell once again displayed his preference for an Imperial alliance and Castillon complained to Henry of his minister's 'great Spanish passion', thus attracting upon Cromwell's head renewed reproofs from the King. In a revealing phrase, the latter told Cromwell that he was a good manager, but not fit to intermeddle in the affairs of kings.

This time, however, the situation did not develop in such a manner as immediately to justify the royal policy of detachment, since in the summer of 1538 Francis and Charles made the Truce of Nice and met in unaccustomed friendship at Aigues Mortes. Marshal de Montmorency, the leading soldier of France, was known to be urging his master to ally with Charles in a joint invasion of England. While Henry continued to anticipate that the two would soon drift apart, Cromwell, who had the task of preparing the country against possible invasion, did not share this optimism. He was ever the tidy-minded administrator, highly responsible, anxious to tame the future, determined to leave nothing to chance. His genius operated most effectively in the field of domestic affairs, where the willed and calculated effect could often be secured, but in that of foreign policy, then as now, gambles had to be taken and hunches obeyed. Masterly inactivity often rewarded England, however dark the reports, for the complexion of Europe changed swiftly enough to make a short-term and opportunist policy the wisest. So often may we observe this antithesis between opportunism and doctrinairism in the chequered story of Tudor diplomacy. Always the opportunists like Henry VII and Elizabeth emerge unscathed, while the doctrinaires, the would-be builders of systems like Wolsey and Mary Tudor, end in confusion. Henry VIII and Cromwell both stood somewhere between the extremes, but the latter leaned somewhat towards the doctrinaires. He had to organize insular defence, but he found it difficult to conceive of a purely insular policy, whereby England would neglect foreign alliances, even one with the ruler of the Netherlands, that integral part of our economy.

Debarred again from an effort to re-establish this old connection by an alliance with the Emperor, he now proceeded to revive the plan for a closer understanding with the Lutheran princes. There was nothing inconsistent in turning from a union with Charles to a union with the enemies of Charles. In Merriman's words, 'As he had always considered the friendship of the Emperor more valuable than that of Francis, so he considered his enmity, which he now regarded as inevitable, as more to be feared'. This being so, what could serve better than an alliance with the princes who, especially with English help, could check the Emperor and prevent his using military or economic weapons against England? Like Walsingham and others after his time, Cromwell wanted to see English battles fought by foreigners on the Continent; indeed, it is not purely fanciful to draw an analogy between him and Pitt, with the German princes cast for the role of Frederick the Great. But in so dignifying Cromwell, we should also give similar credit to his master, who was also a forward-looker, plainly conscious of the protection conferred upon us by control of the Narrow Seas, and an active planner of our growing naval power. Between King and minister we see in embryo the subject of many a future debate, the debate forced upon successive generation of Englishmen until, in our own day, the rise of air-power has revolutionized the major conditions, hitherto prescribed by physical geography and the mobility of armed forces.

Early in 1538 Cromwell prevailed on Henry to send Christopher Mont back to Germany, with the result that by May a Lutheran embassy arrived in England headed by Franz Burckhard, Vice-Chancellor of Saxony. The negotiations were nevertheless speedily bogged down again in theological discussion. It seems likely enough that Cromwell, left to his own plan, would have been quite satisfied with a doctrinal treaty close to the Lutheran position, trusting to uphold it at home through the enhanced strength of the Crown and the harsh lessons recently administered to rebellious conservatives. Henry, on the contrary, was only too relieved when he discovered that the armed preparations of the Emperor were to be directed not against himself but against the Turks. Seeing hence no immediate need of the stubborn Lutherans, he sent the embassy home again in October with the message that an alliance needed maturer deliberation, and that to accomplish it a second embassy would be required. Cromwell, who had merely managed to prevent him from breaking off negotiations altogether, should at this new rebuff have left the King to his own devices in the field of foreign affairs. Instead, he prepared to revive his pressures at the earliest opportunity, and new events soon conspired to provide one. In January 1539 Charles and Francis met at Toledo and agreed not to make any new alliance or marriage-compact with Henry, unless by each other's consent. Cromwell, who had been using the interval to amuse himself with a somewhat chimerical plan for a league of Italian princes against the Pope, once again persuaded Henry to send off the indefatigable Mont on a fresh visit to John Frederick of Saxony, Philip of Hesse and other Schmalkaldic leaders. The supplementary instructions given by Cromwell to Mont make it clear that he was now striving to lift the discussion out of its sterile theological channels and to concentrate upon two proposed dynastic marriages, one between the young Duke William of Cleves and the Princess Mary, the other between Henry himself and Anne, the elder of the same Duke's unmarried sisters.

The choice of the Cleves family supplies an important hint as to the limitations of the Protestant element in Cromwell's foreign policy, for its members were as yet Catholics and not, as so often stated, professed Lutherans. Whatever the desire of the minister to hold the King to a continuing forward policy in religion, his chief interest lay in the political aspects of the alliance rather than in luring the King towards a public display of Protestant sympathies. But if the Catholic allegiance of the House of Cleves made it more acceptable to Henry, the proposed marriages would certainly form a bridge between England and the Schmalkaldic League, since the Duke of Saxony, who had himself married Sybilla, elder sister of Duke William and Anne, stood on intimate terms with the family and had even promised to supply the doweries of his wife's younger sisters. Circumstances had conspired in other ways to confer a considerable diplomatic and strategic lustre upon Cleves. Its late Duke, who died just as these negotiations opened, had built up a centralized administration in his three provinces of Cleves, Jülich and Berg. Moreover, his son and successor William had recently been left the neighbouring province of Gelderland by its childless ruler; at which point the Emperor, reasserting his own claims to that province, had driven Cleves to the protection of Saxony and the Schmalkaldic League. Again, the Cleves lands lay between Charles in the Netherlands and the Lutheran princes whom he wished to attack. For a minister who wanted Henry to operate a North German alliance so as to gain a close grip upon the Netherlands and upon Imperial policy, the Cleves matches must have seemed a heaven-sent opportunity.

The mental calculations of Cromwell beyond this point remain somewhat obscure. He must clearly have foreseen the reverse of these advantages: the danger that England might be committing herself to armed intervention, or at least to squander that immense treasure which he was even now pouring into the royal coffers. We do not know precisely how he planned to steer clear of these abysses. The fact remains that at this stage of his career he thrust ahead, pulling his reluctant master behind him. Did he for once lose his habitual caution and experience a measure of *hubris*? Did he become doctrinaire to the extent of wanting to make his policy look consistent and homogeneous by means of a Lutheran alliance? Did he want the satisfaction of forcing Henry to take medicine which he, Cromwell, thought so obviously good for Henry? Was he applying the old proverb make or mar to new and chancier fields? Had he by now absorbed the Machiavellian concept of *virtù*, the idea that Fortune like a woman gives herself to the bold, that by a superior resolution the great man can control at least that half of his future which does not lie in the lap of Destiny? Whatever the correct answers to these questions, the negotiations for the Cleves match represent a major turning-point of Cromwell's career.

It was naturally to the family friend and protector John Frederick of Saxony that Christopher Mont was ordered to address his first enquiries. Cromwell's further instructions were most circumspect. Having discreetly enquired regarding the shape, stature, proportion, complexion, learning, activity, behaviour and honest qualities of the Lady Anne, Mont should not then crudely demand her, but merely stir the Saxons to 'offer her, as the noblest and highest honour that could come into that noble house of Cleves, if they could bring it to pass'. That Henry himself took pains to preserve a personal loophole becomes ob-

162

vious from the fact that all the material parts of the negotiation were conducted solely in Cromwell's name. Nevertheless, a further worsening of our relations with France and with the Empire encouraged the over-confident minister to press on with the scheme. At this time he was working with immense industry to put the ever-rusting defences of England into some sort of order: his state-papers become littered with muster rolls, weapons, ammunition, provisions and reports on coast-defence. Throughout the country, general musters were held and beacons prepared. Cromwell even took the French ambassador on a tour of the royal armoury and let fall the staggering aside that the King had twenty others as good and better, 'whereat he wondered and said that he thought your Grace the prince the best furnished thereof in Christendom'.

This tension relaxed somewhat in March 1539 when Francis sent his new ambassador Marillac, but the rejoicings at the English court seem childish enough, and Cromwell himself no doubt guessed what we now know: that Francis had not relaxed his hostile intentions and was merely playing for time. So far as the Germans were concerned, the new overtures began with a repetition of the old story. In April Henry cordially received the Saxon ambassadors Burckhard and Baumbach, but still they came intent to discuss a theological understanding and with very limited powers to negotiate any political alliance. When in May it was heard that the Emperor Charles had signed a truce with the Lutheran princes, the King once again sent home the ambassadors. Not least downcast by the news was Robert Barnes in Hamburg, for he had been successfully working to conciliate that intimate ally of the Lutheran princes, Christian of Denmark, whom he had brought to the point of sending to the English court a joint embassy with Saxony to discuss a political league. By what mysterious access of grace did Barnes, at home the embodiment of indiscretion, make an effective diplomat? This possible embryo of a North European Protestant alliance —the dream of so many generations during the long crisis of Reformation and Counter-Reformation—may be placed amongst the larger concepts of Cromwellian diplomacy, but Cromwell is unlikely ever to have felt it so near his grasp as did the sanguine Barnes, who was now heading for a clash with people much bigger than himself. At this stage came the passing of the reactionary Six Articles, the report of which dismayed not only the Lutheran princes but the House of Cleves..

In the summer of 1539 the ever-fluctuating scene brought both sides a fresh motive for renewing contact. Henry discovered that Francis and Charles were again likely to meet and discuss a coalition against him. The former had invited the Emperor to pass through France in order to repress the rebellious city of Ghent, and his consequent appearance in the Netherlands naturally tormented the Duke of Cleves with fears lest Charles should proceed to deprive him of Gelderland. While Henry had dropped the unpopular plan to marry his daughter Mary to the Duke, he maintained a mild interest in Anne of Cleves. It is far from certain that Cromwell even allowed him to see the unexciting personal reports which were coming through. Nicholas Wotton depicted a gentle but utterly unaccomplished female, 'for they take it here in Germany for a rebuke and an occasion of lightness that great ladies should be learned or have any knowledge of music . . . your Grace's servant Hans Holbein hath taken the effigies of my lady Anne and the lady Amelye and hath expressed their images very lively.' Unfortunately for Cromwell, Christopher Mont accorded Anne indiscriminate praise, and while the famous Holbein portrait now in the Louvre is no aphrodisiac, it does at least omit the traces of smallpox which less respectful eyes were quick to observe. When Henry at last saw the original and married her in January 1540, he had good reason to regret his failure to arrange a parade of suitable candidates in Calais. When, months later, Cromwell was in the Tower and hoping to save his skin by helping Henry to a divorce, he wrote a long and curious report of conversations between himself and the King, in which the latter, with much more frankness than taste, had reported his aversion from Anne and his consequent failure to consummate the match. Cromwell had obvious motives for exaggerating these stories, but the details are precise and are partially supported by a letter from Anne to her brother.

In any event, the King did not visit the fallen minister in prison and is not very likely to have dictated details so intimate through a third person. Whatever the case, the failure of Cromwell's political scheme became apparent almost as swiftly as the King's personal aversion. Even amid the continuing hostility of the great powers, the Lutherans staunchly demanded a doctrinal understanding and Henry as staunchly rejected it. On 12 January, 1540, Cromwell summoned Burckhard and Baumbach, who were both again in London, and demanded point-blank a political alliance. The Lutherans were again compelled by their orders to stress the impossibility of such a step in the absence of theological agreement. Cromwell at this point observed that, wherever his personal sympathies might lie, he must hold to his King's belief even to the point of death. Before the end of the month, Henry politely dismissed Baumbach, boasting that he stood in no danger from Charles and Francis, and that in any case his naval strength was more than adequate to meet any opposition it would be likely to encounter. And what use would German soldiers be to him, for they would always be seasick?

This touch of heavy humour did not make the King's mood less dangerous, and Cromwell now realized the necessity of dropping the Lutherans. But he could not spirit away the all-too-solid form of Anne, or escape from the menacing fact that, like Wolsey before him, he had jockeyed the King along a path with a dead end. It is certainly untrue that in January 1540 his death-warrant was sealed, or that an ill-fated foreign policy was solely responsible for his downfall. Even so, the ultimate significance of these events cannot be minimized: not only did they profoundly annoy the irascible King, but they also identified Cromwell ever more clearly with the Lutheran cause and made it far easier for his enemies to press those charges of heresy which proved their sharpest weapons in the final assault. From this point, no further threatening developments on the Continent furnished Cromwell with an excuse for his actions. By February the need to achieve a German alliance had quite plainly receded, since after crushing Ghent Charles repudiated his promise to invest the son of Francis with the Duchy of Milan. Not only did the Emperor thus re-open the old quarrel with France; he also reasserted his claim to Gelderland, hence making it all too likely that Cleves and the Lutherans would call upon Henry for practical support, a prospect from which the King recoiled in dismay. Shortly before Cromwell's arrest in June, Henry sent an emissary to Charles in Brussels, assuring him that Cromwell had exceeded his instructions and placing upon Cromwell's shoulders the blame for negotiating with the Lutheran princes.

It is now high time to take up the threads in domestic affairs which also led to the Reaction and to the fall of Cromwell. They are no less complex than those we have traced in the sphere of foreign policy. The likelihood had always existed that, when the policy of Reformation reached a certain climax, it would receive a violent check. The intrinsic weakness of the Cromwell-Cranmer group amongst the nobility and the bishops, even amongst the predominantly conservative squirearchy and the agrarian masses, need not again be stressed. But the timing and the severity of such a reaction depended upon the King, whose personal friendship towards Cranmer and whose reliance upon Cromwell's administrative genius were props he could not and would not lightly discard. In the summer of 1539, certain observers thought the moment had already arrived, for it was then that the first gaps were torn in the Cromwellian front by the Duke of Norfolk and the conservative bishops. But the sequel indicated that the King was not nearly prepared for a change of ministry.

When the new Parliament assembled on 28 April, Cromwell had on his list of impending measures 'a devise for the unity in religion', but the King had evidently given him no precise indication of its form. The committee set up in the Lords at Henry's request was headed by the Vicegerent, but it consisted of four Reformers (Cranmer, Latimer, Goodrich of Ely and Capon of Bangor) and four conservatives (Lee of York, Tunstall, Clerk of Bath and Wells and Aldridge of Carlisle); the King may even have intended the inevitable deadlock, which enabled him to assume personal control as *deus ex machina*. On 16 May he authorized the Duke of Norfolk to offer six articles to Parliament for discussion: as yet they stood in the form of questions, but they were questions to which Henry now knew the answers. It may be that while Cromwell was immersed in committee-business, Norfolk and Gardiner had captured the King's ear, but Henry's own grasp and enthusiasm cannot be doubted. Not only did he revise the first extant draft of the Six Articles Act in his own hand, but he soon came down in person to the debate and, as a conservative lord put it, 'confounded them all with God's learning'. The very exclusion of the Vicegerent from the task of introducing an important religious measure boded no good to Cromwell and his policy. When Parliament reassembled after a week's prorogation, Gardiner emerged from the wings and joined one of the committees formed to draft the Act, which during June passed through all its stages. Cromwell naturally submitted to the strong lead of the King, while doing what he could to mitigate some of the harsher provisions. Even so, the final terms of the Act proved wholeheartedly conservative and its penalties violent in the extreme. It asserted transubstantiation and condemned those who denied this doctrine to burning and to forfeiture of all property, without possibility of escape by abjuration. The other five articles stated that communion in both kinds for the laity was unnecessary, since the whole Christ was present in both bread and wine; that the law of God prevented priests from marriage and demanded the continued observance of vows of chastity; that private masses should continue and that auricular confession was expedient and necessary. For obstinate denial of any of these five, a man should be judged a felon and so suffer death and forfeiture, but in the event of abjuration, he should be imprisoned at the King's pleasure, and suffer death only if twice convicted.

At this stage, Cromwell stood face to face with something more formidable than a mere clerical reaction. The lay lords headed by Norfolk had played a predominant part in the passage of this fierce Act, while a considerable section of the lower orders, their normal conservatism reinforced by the spectacle of religious disunity in the realm, did not hesitate to rejoice at the strong line taken by King and Parliament. In London itself, according to Hall, five hundred persons were speedily presented for heresy under the Act. At the same time, the outcome showed that the Six Articles were intended—like most Tudor penal legislation—to operate as a deterrent rather than as basis for a close inquisition into the nation's conscience. So far as Foxe's information went, only about 25 persons were actually burned under the Act during the last eight years of the reign. The immediate political consequences likewise proved undramatic. Only two of the Reforming bishops—Shaxton and Latimer—resigned their secs, and Latimer afterwards alleged that he did so at Cromwell's own request. And distressed as Cromwell himself must have been at this triumph of reaction, he soon found that Henry still valued his services. During the second half of 1539 he recovered his influence and, as already observed, went ahead with the Cleves match. The Act also failed to put Gardiner into a significantly more powerful position. Cromwell continued to hold him at a distance from the King, while the new appointments to the episcopal bench did not come from Gardiner's faction. Capon and Bell, who succeeded Shaxton and Latimer, were moderates, while Bonner, who became Bishop of London on Stokesley's death in the autumn, remained a bitter personal enemy of Gardiner and a Cromwellian up to the time of the minister's fall.

So matters substantially remained until the early months of 1540 saw a further shift of the front. Norfolk's special embassy to France in February provides an interesting link between foreign affairs and the intrigue for power at home: Norfolk had everything to gain by staging a reconciliation with France, since this diminished the need for Cromwell's German alliance and increased the impatience of the King with the match he had just been led to make. But again, Norfolk's success in March did not in itself entail Cromwell's fall, an event which cannot closely be synchronized with the foreign situation. At home threats more dangerous were developing. In this same month the minister suffered grave embarrassment from the behaviour of Barnes, who, home again and flushed with his diplomatic successes, lost touch with life's stern realities and made a violent attack upon Gardiner in a sermon at Paul's Cross. On the Bishop's protest, the King called the disputants before him and ordered Barnes to confer with his adversary. The Reformer at first professed himself convinced, and was even offered a fat benefice by the elated Gardiner. Yet within two days Barnes rushed in disillusion from the bishop's palace, only to be summoned again before the King, together with his two chief associates William Jerome and Thomas Garret, that early hero of Oxford Protestantism. Ordered by Henry to preach sermons of recantation, they complied in so unsatisfactory a manner as to gain for themselves cells in the Tower. Their defiance culminated on 30 March, when Barnes withdrew his recantation.

These events delighted Norfolk and no doubt correspondingly depressed Cromwell, yet the latter took care to avoid any gesture of sympathy for Barnes and his friends. On the day of Barnes's fatal sermon, Cromwell was in fact dining with Gardiner in a supreme effort to come to terms with that insidious enemy, whom the King was about to recall to the Council. Gardiner allowed Cromwell to think the dinner and discussion a success, yet he implacably awaited the moment to strike. On 10 April the French ambassador Marillac was already prophesying Cromwell's imminent fall: he had noted the imprisonment of the three Protestant divines and the appearance upon the Council of the three conservative bishops, Gardiner, Tunstall and Clerk. Once again the prophecy was premature, for on 12 April Cromwell opened the parliamentary session with a nobly-worded plea for mutual toleration and charity, while six days later he was created Earl of Essex and Great Chamberlain, with substantial grants to maintain his dignities. Even the common suggestion that the King was merely preserving him until he had negotiated the subsidy bill and the confiscation of the properties of the order of St. John does not agree with the dates, since he survived some little time after these measures had safely passed through Parliament. Meanwhile ecclesiastical affairs were again slipping from his grasp, since the committee appointed to define doctrine was heavily loaded with conservatives.

In May the trap was gradually closing; faced by the task of delivering Henry from Anne of Cleves, he was now confronted with the certainty that, as soon as he succeeded, Henry would marry Katherine Howard, Norfolk's niece, whom the wily Duke had carefully planted under the roving eye of the King. Before the end of the month Cromwell had abandoned his restraint to the extent of arresting on his own responsibility Gardiner's lieutenants, Sampson Bishop of Chichester and Dr. Nicholas Wilson. It was rumoured that he planned to seize five more conservative bishops, but while he was again immersed in parliamentary routine, Norfolk and Gardiner succeeded in convincing the suspicious King that he was guilty of heresy and treason. The long intrigue ended on 10 June, when the captain of the guard came to arrest him in the Council Chamber. Taken by surprise, and doubtless filled by the furious thought that he had not completed his task, the victim hurled his bonnet to the ground in rage, called on his enemies to say if he were a traitor, and then urged them to dispose of him quickly and not leave him to linger. Norfolk snatched the George from his neck and Southampton the Garter from his knee; the councillors, a few moments ago conformable to his leadership, joined in the storm of vituperation as the fallen statesman was taken by boat to the Tower. No one save Cranmer, and he very cautiously, dared express regret or recall past friendship with Cromwell in the presence of the King. By the evening, archers guarded the door of his house, while inside men packed his plate and money for the King's use. This was the accepted sign that a man would die.

The last scene in the Council Chamber serves to remind us of another important influence behind the triumph of reaction. Dr. Elton has recently shown that the development and complexion of the Privy Council itself were important factors in the downfall of Cromwell. The Council had now become a compact and efficient body which rendered a single super-minister no longer essential. It contained, however, no Cromwellian group of ministers likely to support their leader in time of crisis; he had never manned it with his personal adherents and it was united only by loyalty and subservience to the King. Such colleagues as Tunstall, Southampton, Browne and Kingston were unconcealed conservatives in religion. Lord Russell and Chancellor Audley, ostensibly close friends of the minister, were Cromwellian only by self-interest and prepared to drop their leader at the slightest breath of royal disfavour. His own former servant Ralph Sadler naturally concentrated upon self-preservation when Cromwell's power began to totter. In April Cromwell had relinquished the secretaryship to Sadler and Wriothesley, but if his motive was to bring more of his own associates to the Council, he did not in fact receive any appreciable access of strength at these hands. Grounds in fact exist for the supposition that Wriothesley worked behind Cromwell's back for his overthrow; certainly this unpleasing character became on Cromwell's fall an eminent member of the Norfolk–Gardiner reactionary group. This being the case, Cromwell's situation bore little resemblance to that of a modern Prime Minister. To avert or mitigate the disfavour of the King he had not even a phalanx of sympathetic officers of state, let alone a parliamentary party, behind him. The service of a suspicious monarch had created in the governing group an atmosphere devoid of generosity, fair play, friendship and any loyalty except to Sovereign and to self. When Cromwell fell, it suited his critics to depict him as the creator of this merciless atmosphere, and many a historian has foolishly accepted the charge at its face-value. Indeed, from the viewpoint of self-preservation he had woefully lacked ruthlessness. Unmoved, he had watched subservient juries condemn more or less harmless monks, but he had not sought, while he had the chance, to lay those elaborate traps which would have destroyed his real enemies. With the powerful he had preferred hospitality and persuasion. When their turn came, Norfolk and Gardiner knew better; they knew that 'stone dead hath no fellow', and they disdained to utilize no lie, however fantastic, if it served the purpose of his destruction.

The Attainder originally introduced in the Lords on 17 June

was afterwards dropped in favour of another version drawn up in the Commons, the one finally passed by the end of the month. The charges rehearsed against Cromwell seem at least as monstrous as those brought in former years against the most innocent of the conservatives. The methods of his accusers are best illustrated by their initial search for someone who would swear that in 1538 Cromwell had announced he would make himself King and marry the Princess Mary. Some of the accusations actually retained seem little less amazing. As the Act stands, the chief author seems to be Norfolk, since it dwells so repeatedly on the fact that Cromwell had been of poor and low degree, 'as few be within this your realm', and relates that, when reminded of these low origins, he had replied that 'if the lords would handle him so, that he would give them such a breakfast as never was made in England, and that the proudest should know'. We are powerfully reminded of Lord Darcy's prophecy. Hall ascribed Cromwell's fall chiefly to his offence against the 'snoffing pride of some prelates', but he also fell because in the service of the State he had never taken blue blood at more than its intrinsic worth. Of the major charges, the less serious relate to an alleged misuse of powers by acting without the King's consent; the more serious are charges of heresy. The first group was wisely kept vague: he had set at liberty people suspected of treason or attainted of misprision; he had sold licences to aliens to export money and goods; he had set up commissions without the King's knowledge; he had pretended to have power over the King; he had given passports to aliens without the King's consent. Such charges proved easy to make against a minister with such a range of powers and duties. As Cromwell himself readily admitted, 'I have meddled in so many matters under your Highness that I am not able to answer them all'.

The heresy-charges were only a shade more precise. Being a detestable heretic and utterly disposed to sow common sedition and variance amongst the King's true and loving subjects (perhaps the most astonishing phrase in the document!), Cromwell had spread heretical literature, caused heretical writings to be translated, and had asserted it lawful for every Christian man to minister the sacrament. As Vicegerent he had licensed heretics to preach and teach, had set them at liberty, refused to listen to accusations against them, and in order more firmly to establish heresies, had drawn to himself 'by retainours' many whom he infected. Finally, someone was found to swear that on 31 March 1539, he had said in the parish of St. Peter the Poor that the teaching of Barnes and other heretics was good and that, even if the King would turn from it, he himself would not, but would fight in the field sword-in-hand against the King and all others. Bishop Burnet later remarked with justice that had Cromwell really uttered such sentiments, Bedlam would have been a fitter place for his restraint than the Tower.

No wonder his enemies resolved to proceed by Act of Attainder, since this precluded court-proceedings in which the most incompetent defendant could have revealed the absurdity of such charges. Judging by Cromwell's letter to the King, the men who testified to verbal treasons were Sir George Throgmorton and Sir Richard Riche, Chancellor of the Augmentations. These names, as Dr. Elton has remarked, destroy any lingering belief that the charges were true. Throgmorton had been a prominent critic of the divorce; he was the brother of Pole's chief lieutenant and a well-known enemy of Cromwell. Riche was the witness who had already perjured himself to produce evidence of verbal treason against Sir Thomas More. In his letter of 12 June to the King, Cromwell protested that he never remembered speaking to these two together and that, 'if I did, I am sure I spake never of any such matter: and your Grace knoweth what manner of man Throgmorton hath ever been towards your Grace and your proceedings; and what Master Chancellor (Riche) hath been towards me, God and he best knoweth'. If Henry stopped to read these words, he might well have hesitated before executing a minister on such testimony; perhaps he remembered its character when, so soon afterwards, he came to see how he had been deceived.

This first letter of Cromwell is full of outraged and transparent declarations of loyalty, somewhat lost in the pedantically unpunctuated edition of Merriman. 'For as I ever', he exclaims, 'have had love to your honour, person, life, prosperity, health, wealth, joy and comfort, and also your most dear and most entirely beloved son the Prince his Grace, and your proceedings, God so help me in this mine adversity, and confound me if ever I thought the contrary! What labours, pains and travails I have taken according to my most bounden duty, God also knoweth; for if it were in my power, as it is God's, to make your Majesty to live ever young and prosperous, God knoweth I would. If it had been or were in my power to make you so rich as ye might enrich all men, God help me as I would do it. If it had been or were in my power to make your Majesty so puissant as all the world should be compelled to obey you, Christ he knoweth I would, for so am I of all other most bound, for your Majesty hath been the most bountiful prince to me that ever was King to his subject; yea, and more like a dear father (your Majesty not offended) than a master.'

The second letter from the Tower, that of 30 June, is much less dignified and moving, for it is the one in which he reports the evidence concerning the King's early relations with Anne of Cleves. The interval had also emboldened him to think there might be a remote chance of playing upon Henry's sentiments. While he professes himself 'ready to take the death when it shall please God and your Majesty', he continues, 'and yet the frail flesh inciteth me continually to call to your Grace for mercy and pardon for mine offences'. And at the end of his letter he adds: 'Most gracious prince, I cry for mercy, mercy, mercy'. This ejaculation has inevitably been taken out of its context to show that Cromwell made a squalid end, which he did not. Most political prisoners of the period used these tactics, and Tudor manners did not inculcate the concealment of natural emotions. Moreover, quite unlike Sir Thomas More, Cromwell had every reason to think of his death as senseless, for it vindicated no principle and seemed to leave a task manifestly incomplete. When the last hour arrived, it was likewise in keeping with contemporary manners that on the scaffold the condemned offender should make an improving, loyal, resigned and religious oration. Not infrequently its sense was remembered, written up and embellished by admirers. On 28 July, his long wait ended, Cromwell made such a speech and apparently made it well, though the beautiful oration and prayer put by Hall and Foxe into the mouth of 'this valiant soldier and captain of Christ' are no more verbally authentic than those assigned to their heroes by the great historians of Antiquity and of the Renaissance. So, concludes Foxe, 'he patiently suffered the stroke of the axe, by a ragged, butcherly miser, which very ungodly performed the office'. And so, he might justly have added, there passed from the scene the most devoted, laborious and efficient servant of the Crown in the long history of England.

Chapter Eleven

Modern Perspectives

HISTORIANS have commonly overestimated the statesmanship and originality of Henry VIII, and in consequence have underrated those of Thomas Cromwell. Even so, the King's services to the nation may still in retrospect be considered great. When the dangers of relapse into anarchy had by no means subsided, one cannot regret that a great and masterful personality came to occupy the throne. Despite his fits of inhumanity against individuals, he bestowed upon the short and troubled lives of Tudor men and women the incalculable blessing of a long internal peace, and upon his work was founded the even longer Elizabethan peace. Bearing in mind the too often hideous fate of Continental common men in the age of the so-called wars of religion, it would be no exaggeration to call Henry a true friend of the common Englishman. Yet this stabilizing and restraining role of the King can scarcely be dubbed creative. Ever in ultimate control, Henry prescribed the conditions and boundaries within which more original and industrious minds might operate, yet he himself neither generated nor consistently released the forces of change. It seems a matter of demonstrable fact that all the great constructive and destructive achievements of his long reign were crowded into the brief eight years of Thomas Cromwell's ministry. Even if we knew nothing in detail concerning the minister's personal responsibilities, it would be impossible to regard the phenomenon as pure coincidence. In comparison with this concentrated series of decisive actions, the rest of the reign looks at best a holding-operation, so much of its spectacular effort being in the last resort sterile. Henry's personal creativeness may be fairly judged by the achievements of his last six years, when he held his ministers and subjects in a grip of unprecedented firmness, yet dissipated quite inconclusively the immense resources which Cromwell had placed in his hands. No part of his reign comes so near to deserving the reproach of failure.

Within the Cromwellian years, the spectacle is marvellous even where it is unattractive. It abounds in new ideas, still more in sheer political and administrative energy. The dead weight of ancient routines and ideas is hurled aside with a radicalism all the more remarkable in that Cromwell, unlike his namesake and unlike Napoleon, had to hand no rich stock of revolutionary doctrines. The statesman we have just glimpsed in a Reformation context was also the director of innumerable activities external or peripheral to our subject. Few administrative schemes, for example, have exerted more interesting effects upon the religious and intellectual history of Britain than the new *régime* established by Cromwell in Wales. His statutes culminated in the dissolution of the turbulent Marcher lordships, the complete shiring of the country, the reception of English law, conciliar government, justices of the peace and parliamentary representation. Alongside these steps went Rowland Lee's ruthless campaign against crime and disorder. The wisdom of this policy, in which Cromwell persisted when even Lee feared it might be premature, is in no way impugned by those evils which sprang from the neglect of Welsh problems by later governments. Though Cromwell cannot have foreseen the less direct results of his measures, he showed a firm and conscious grasp of the creative nature of social order, a principle never demonstrated to greater advantage than in Wales. The criticisms of Welsh parochialists, ever oblivious to the true achievements of their own expansive nation, should not be directed against the reformer who set free a small yet highly gifted nation to influence, enliven and diversify far larger societies. In particular, the subsequent history of British religion, both at home and abroad, would be as unthinkable without its Welsh components as without those which in later generations emanated from the Scots.

That the experience of Wales was no accident of history may be seen in the parallel experience of northern England, where Cromwell refashioned the King's Council in the North and made it function effectively for the first time in its history. Here Robert Holgate (another able ecclesiastic dubbed by the romantics 'a creature of Cromwell') began to change another lawless and faction-ridden people into one of the most energetic and purposeful sections of English society. When a worthy life of Cromwell comes to be written, it will devote many pages to the statesmanship which broke the feudal liberties and the sanctuaries, repressed the family factions, maintained peace and even co-operation with the Scots, promoted the overthrow of the Geraldines in Ireland, began the series of national poor-laws and removed the focus of the cloth-trade from Antwerp to London. It may devote even more to the Cromwell who stopped the debasement and export of the coinage, solved by one statute the old problem of Uses, remoulded and expanded the national system of financial courts, made the Principal Secretary chief minister in place of the Chancellor, and perfected the development of the small and workmanlike Privy Council. In the field of the State, he was indeed a true 'universal man' of the Renaissance. That there existed a personal and opportunist element in some of these changes cannot be denied; it could not be otherwise when so much of the drive and the supervision came from a single man surrounded by rivals, and never permitted a pause for the consolidation and delegation of authority. Yet unlike Wolsey, Cromwell was a Pygmalion whose creations had a strange power to develop a vitality of their own, one which in many cases long outlasted the brief rule of their author. Not all his labours were proof against the incapacity of his successors, yet in general their survival-value proved high, because they possessed administrative logic and corresponded with the needs of that day and the next.

Behind the complexities of detail, Cromwell's policy looks highly coherent: his work is all of a piece and bears a personal signature. In his Reformation-policy, just as in all other spheres, he was first and foremost a state-builder. The significance of the English Reformation is very far from being limited to religious or even to ecclesiastical history: it is a crisis and a resolution of crisis in the history of the English State and people. It forms a crucial chapter in the story of our sovereignty, of our national law and institutions, of our psychological responses to the claims of authority. The main result of the Cromwellian phase was the transfer of the great ecclesiastical sector of English society and law to the sovereignty of the King in Parliament. And if this transfer belongs to the rise of Leviathan, the fact should be judged neither in our present-day context nor even in a Hobbesian context, since in mid-Tudor times the need to strengthen the State was far stronger than at any later phase of English history. Oliver Cromwell was chiefly concerned to wrest the helm of the ship from incompetent steersmen, but Thomas Cromwell had to repair the rotten timbers of the ship itself. In his day, Englishmen were not choosing between autocracy and democracy; they were choosing between a powerful State and intermittent anarchy. By no means every detailed step of the Cromwellian Reformation can be justified by reference to such needs, yet the whole transaction belongs to the story of the nation in its broadest aspects: it can never be understood by narrowly ecclesiastical historians.

In the international sphere, Cromwell has obvious significance as a leading agent in the severance of Englishmen from the ancient papal bond and from the ideal of an international Christendom. The strictly doctrinal aspects of this step must be left to theologians. Regarding its political and cultural implications, we have already recorded the view that these have been commonly exaggerated, that More's idealism meant little in terms of international peace, justice, brotherhood and freedom, that the revolt of the northern nations against a Mediterranean-centred Church had now—irrespective of mere personalities—become practically inevitable. Cromwell's intellectual limitations appear less in his rejection of a dubious internationalism than in the *naïveté* which made him see in Rome, rather than in Spain, the detested centre of a system in which English interests must always suffer betrayal. Yet he was neither the creator of the English insular tradition nor the inventor of a radically new foreign policy. While opposed to wasteful jingoism, he retained the anti-French prejudices of his generation. Again in an established medieval tradition, he strove hard to maintain peace with the ruler of the Netherlands. Failing this, he sought to organize alliances in Germany. Personally well-travelled and highly cautious, he represents the less insular of the two moods of subsequent English foreign policy.

Greater ultimate significance attaches to Cromwell's part in the evolution of erastian principles; in the emergence at home of a lay-dominated society with its mind firmly fixed upon moderation, good sense and security in this world. Not for Englishmen the superb follies of Spain's self-martyrdom to a fanatic ideal. Even less did they want to see other-worldly aspirations used to justify internal anarchy and bloodshed. Before the harsh experience of civil war had impressed similar lessons upon Bodin and the *Politiques* in France, Englishmen, clerical and lay alike, rejected the primacy of doctrinal allegiances, preferred peace to a sword and embraced the vision of a paternal state, harsh against traitors yet mild towards heretics. The early stages of this process may with all the greater confidence be ascribed to Cromwell and his group, since the King himself seems to have understood its implications none too clearly. If from one angle Cromwell was a careerist who sold the King a revolutionary plan to gain his divorce, his far-seeing mind obviously penetrated beyond these mere occasons and implements of change to the concept of a more efficiently and rationally organized nation, one based not merely upon administrative and judicial reforms, but upon a new triangular relationship between Church, State and Society. Worldly security is not an ideal which can be freely impugned by our own generation. Those who criticize the erastian programme as earthy and mundane would not themselves prefer to have lived in an England torn by pseudo-religious strife. Such critics should reflect that Tudor men and women were no mere stepping-stones towards our noble selves, that they did not exist to provide us with colourful spectacles, or even with the prototypes of modern liberal democracy. Unavoidable circumstance made their lives harsh and short; their small share of ease and amenity depended in large part upon royal justice and the peace of the commonwealth. Here they had emphatically no reason to envy either foreigners or their own forebears.

In retrospect Cromwell stands out as the leader of an invasion of our public affairs by laymen and the lay spirit. He and his like show a vivid consciousness of the shortcomings of ecclesiastical administration and jurisdiction; behind the thin facade of courteous reverence, they entertained a strong resentment against the professional *esprit de corps,* the easily-won wealth, the hauteur and fundamental worldliness of their prelatical associates. No fair-minded observer would deny that much hypocrisy marked this lay invasion. It was accompanied by too much greed and self-interest. Given a juster vision, its exponents might also have concentrated a part of their reforming zeal against the penal ferocity, the inequities, the corruptions from which even lay justice had yet by no means liberated itself. Too few of them showed either Cromwell's penchant for rationalization, or the ardour of the Commonwealth Party for economic and social reform. Yet though the lay invasion was not executed by angels of light, some of its results might now be reasonably defended——even by churchmen! Throughout its long history the Christian Church has often been corrupted by worldly power, and as often, to its ultimate benefit, been struck down in judgement. By the reign of Henry VIII, the incapacity of the English Church to achieve self-reform had too long invited interference by its lay members and by their clerical allies. Yet the radicalism of the changes they thrust upon it has commonly been exaggerated. Cromwell did not, for example, seek to destroy ecclesiastical jurisdiction. As the records of any diocesan registry prove, the church courts survived his ministry intact; their methods underwent no significant modifications; their control over the lives of both clergy and laity showed no sudden or dramatic decline throughout the Tudor age. It was an evolutionary process which turned the national Church from judicial and coercive into persuasive and missionary habits of mind. Again, the lay revolution was to a surprising extent executed by clergymen. They were critical rather than Protestant, and they provided Cromwell with some of his ablest agents. Such men as Rowland Lee, Robert Holgate, Edward Fox and Thomas Starkey have inevitably been castigated as renegades—inevitably, but in general unjustly, for they believed in what they were doing, and grasped the simple point that ecclesiastical and social reforms were unlikely to be initiated by any other agency save the State. Cromwell spent a large part of his career working with clergymen; he never allowed his anticlericalism to interfere with his use of the best available talent and conviction. It might indeed be more accurate to describe the Cromwellian movement as anti-prelatical rather than anticlerical, for while the lower clergy took his reforms as they came, the bishops never looked quite the same again.

In this story of Cromwell's alliance with the critical forces of society, the Protestants play a somewhat dubious role. He became notorious as the protector of numerous individual Reformers; despite his apparent lack of spiritual ardour, it looks as if previous historians have not taken his religious convictions with nearly enough seriousness, He showed both temperamental and logical affinities with the Lutherans; he collapsed partly because he had laid himself open to charges of heresy, and had taken risks to build a Protestant confederation; he emerged somewhat startlingly in literature as John Foxe's 'valiant soldier and captain of Christ'. Far more significantly, he ensured the extension of Protestant ideas by giving the English Bible to the people, an action which alone assures him a curious yet conspicuous place in the history of religion proper. For all that, he proffered the Bible to the public in a spirit very different from that which animated men like Foxe. We have already glimpsed a likelihood that the biblical policy was related not only to the anticlerical but to the constructive and educational aspects of his social policy. Between the Bible and erastianism in general, the logical connections seem also obvious. A religion based on scriptural research and exegesis logically demanded a measure of mutual forbearance between the differing schools of interpretation, but where else could this forbearance be ensured save within the framework of State-supremacy? The return of Protestantism to persecuting, conformist and would-be oecumenical notions proceeded to obscure this logic—both inside and outside the Anglican communion—until the nineteenth century. It remains nevertheless a logic explicit enough in the settlement envisaged by Cromwell, who in matters of religion saw the State less as formulating the rules of the game than as a referee duly empowered to keep the players in order. His secular awareness of the limitations of dogmatism, together with the liberal concepts of Melancthon, caused him to stand much nearer to modern tolerationist concepts than did either Henry VIII or Calvin.

Quite apart from these concepts, it is also difficult to exaggerate the importance for English Protestantism of that breathing-space which his ministry provided. These years saw the old orthodoxy lose its last chances of pursuing inquisitorial tactics with a reasonable hope of success. The fact received tacit admission even from Henry VIII, whose political commonsense forbade him to follow Cromwell's death by a Catholic persecution of any great intensity and scope. Yet if Cromwell did much for Protestantism, it was yet neither strong enough nor sufficiently well-led to repay his services. Emphatically, he did not ride to power upon a wave of Protestant sentiment, and if he ever anticipated massive political support from a fast-growing Protestant body, he must have been sorely disappointed. The English Bible apart, his ecclesiastical enterprises might have been pursued with equal success had Lutheranism never reached England. And could he have foreseen the theocracy about to emerge from Geneva, he might have admired its cult of efficiency, yet he might also have exclaimed, more vociferously than any, that new presbyter was but old priest writ large.

With the origins of Anglicanism his connections appear somewhat more clear-cut. Unspiritual by nature and background, he obviously contributed little to its devotional ethos, but more than any man he supplied it with the less ethereal rudiments of its character: its notion of the *via media*, its institutionalized Supremacy of King in Parliament, its adiaphorist attempt to comprehend divergent doctrinal trends, its valiant effort to be scriptural, its emphases upon patriotism, service to the State, sound learning, public education and good sense, as opposed to strict logic. Throughout the last hundred years, the Anglo-Catholic viewpoint has been predominant in Anglican historiography, and the antipathy of its adherents towards a hard-boiled lay Vicegerent can well be understood. They wanted almost all the results of the Reformation, while detesting the process itself. At the same time, emotion should not have blinded these historians to the creative influences of Thomas Cromwell and of his humanist-clerical assistants, who began to formulate the medial position of the national Church. Even strong doctrinal partisans within the Anglican communion need nowadays feel no shame concerning this early branch of their family tree. If the Cromwellians were neither saints nor martyrs, they did not much resemble the villains of neo-Tractarian melodrama. The growing realization that even Cromwell had his special brand of idealism may help to make him a shade more acceptable even to those who, inspired directly or indirectly by Dixon and Gairdner (if not by Gasquet and Belloc), have hitherto averted their eyes in pained rejection. Cromwell bore an important share in defining the terms upon which a national and imperial Church was to be linked with the State. These inhibiting links have naturally been regarded with impatience by many of its most devoted members. Too often in their warring convictions they have overlooked the corresponding advantages. A Church based upon relatively comprehensive and liberal lines would otherwise soon have been fractured through the efforts of zealots to capture it for their respective schools of thought. Precisely because of its mundane detachment from dogmatic zeal, the State has always tended to enforce this experiment in active toleration which forms the peculiar appeal of Anglicanism. And the greatest spiritual achievements of the Church of England have generally been attained in conjunction with the State and with national secular enterprise.

Amongst the major ecclesiastical schemes of Cromwell, I take the dissolution of the monasteries to have less historical importtance than has commonly been supposed. It may be deposed from its former pre-eminence for many reasons: because the monasteries had already ceased to be an influential force in English life; because monasticism could not in any case have survived in Elizabethan England; because Cromwell's attempt to endow the Crown with monastic revenues was thwarted by the squander-mania of Henry's last years; because it now seems impossible to elevate the social and economic results of the dissolution to the status of a cataclysm in our history. Today no informed students of the period can be impressed by the worthless quotations from Fuller, Spelman, Cobbett and various later sentimentalists, which Gasquet and others have utilized to produce that familiar cataclysmic picture: the wealthy Protestant gentry rack-renting the peasantry and driving men from the land by enclosures; the poor made ever poorer, the monks themselves driven to 'a deplorable life of vagrancy and poverty'. The literary evidence of contemporaries lays an almost negligible emphasis upon the dissolution as a cause of poverty, but even if it had taken the dramatic line, most of it would be worthless, because pamphleteers and pulpit-moralists who did not understand such elementary background-factors at the great inflation cannot claim acceptance as serious economic analysts. At no stage of the Tudor period was the extent of enclosures very large, but they had been a problem recognized by legislation many years before the monastic suppression, while religious houses themselves had not infrequently enclosed to the hurt of their tenants and neighbours. Again, on the present evidence, no spate of rack-renting can be shown to have arisen from the dissolution. In any case, why should tenant-farmers have prospered by the immense mid-Tudor rise in food-prices, while their landlords contented themselves with low, pre-inflationary rents? The silvermines of Peru destroyed long in advance the extremist legends beloved alike by Fabian and Catholic propagandists. And even supposing the monasteries had survived and had suddenly switched to a quixotic policy, by what financial wizardry could they have kept their rents static in an inflationary world?

In one respect, at least, the significance of the dissolution seems little diminished by modern research. It continues to occupy an important place among the factors which, as the Tudor age advanced, rendered the landed gentry a more numerous and a more potent section of English society. From this time a thriving market in land became a continuous feature of the nation's economic life, and over the years land was to prove an excellent investment for most of its purchasers. In any sizeable shire, one may point to several clear examples of families which based a new or a growing prosperity upon wise purchases of monastic and other church lands. Many of these so-called 'new men' were certainly younger sons of established families, though often they attained independent estates through the profits of an official or legal career. Less commonly, it would seem, the newcomers were substantial yeomen, already achieving economic equality with the class they were destined to enter. Less commonly still, in my experience, they were genuinely newcomers with little previous background save that of business or the professions. When we seek to check these broad impressions by detailed reference to regional and local history, the surviving records demand slow and painstaking analysis. It was easy for Savine and Liljegren to make a list of the original grantees of monastic lands drawn from the Patent Rolls; easy, but almost in vain, since little interest attaches to the many transient first buyers who held these lands for very brief periods during the years immediately following the dissolution. With far greater significance, the Particulars for Grants can be made, in the light of local knowledge, to establish the prevalent types of ownership into which the lands fell during the two or three decades between 1540 and the early years of Elizabeth. Such information 'in depth' is well worth having, but as yet it has been presented in full detail only in the case of the county of Devon. Here Dr. Youings has shown that these lands did not pass to a handful of rich men but increased the number of moderate-sized estates. More important, they did not create a new class of profiteer-merchant-landlords, but by 1558 were widely distributed amongst members of established local families, less than 10 per cent. being owned by people who came in from outside Devon. This unsensational picture is in general supported by Mr. Hodgett's researches on the Lincolnshire monastic lands. The groups of London speculators who here initially bought parcels with a view to profitable resale were ephemeral owner. Professor Habakkuk has recently given strong reasons for the belief that many so-called speculators were mere humble agents from whom the real purchasers took over the lands within a short space of time. There seems nowhere evidence to indicate the rise of a novel type of landlord emancipated from the decent usages of rural society. Again, the purchase of monastic lands had nothing to do with doctrinal allegiances, and many of the greatest purchasers were known religious conservatives. Even the widespread notion that the sale of monastic lands guaranteed England against the revival of Catholic doctrine has little to recommend it: not for a moment was Mary's reaction seriously threatened by nervous owners of ex-monastic lands, nor did even this injudicious ruler attempt to make such owners disgorge their unholy purchases. Further research will need to produce many surprises before we can make the dissolution a general scapegoat for pauperism and other social evils, the causes of which can be seen plainly enough in quite different fields of the national economy. All in all, Cromwell's dissolution-policy doubtless represents an injustice towards the monastic ideal; it was certainly a failure, in that it brought no lasting financial stability to the Crown; yet it cannot, on the evidence now available, be supposed to have exerted catastrophic or permanent effects upon the material lives of Englishmen. For the neglect of the Crown to make better use of monastic revenues in the ecclesiastical and educational fields we have already seen the absurdity of blaming Cromwell, who was destroyed when he had scarcely completed the dissolution itself. By a curious irony, so many of the financial plans by which he set such store were fated to be nullified through unforeseen circumstance or by incapable successors.

With such considerations in mind, we should do belated justice to the memory of a great English statesman and patriot by devoting more attention to those fields in which he received some opportunity to follow up his initial reforms and exercise some control over their sequels. In the light of modern knowledge, such elements of his work seem likely to bulk much larger than in the past. To those whose ideals still centre around an international Church, a papal headship and a powerful clerical order, the destructive elements must continue to bulk larger still. Rightly or wrongly, many nations in the western tradition have refused to revert to such ideals, and it is across their histories that the influence of Thomas Cromwell and of his Elizabethan legatees stands most patently inscribed. On some other aspects of his story a growing measure of agreement between Catholics and non-Catholics may remain within the bounds of possibility. I like to presume, for example, that the merely sordid, selfish, cruel careerist has returned for ever into the realm of legend where it belongs, and that Thomas Cromwell's revolutionary conviction, the breadth and bigness of his ideas, are now being reasonably demonstrated. A reader who still doubted his ultimate sincerity, his zeal to 'edify' or create, might turn with profit to that long, heartfelt, even emotional letter which he wrote to Bishop Shaxton during their disagreements in March 1538. It has a strangely convincing ring when the writer declares that he, just as much as any priest, feels himself engaged upon God's work, and that he aims solely at constructive results. 'I do not cease to give thanks that it has pleased His goodness to use me as an instrument and to work somewhat by me, so I trust I am as ready to serve Him in my calling as you are. . . . My prayer is that God give me no longer life than I shall be glad to use mine office in edification and not in destruction.'

Select Bibliography

A. Thomas Cromwell

The *Bibliography of British History*, ed. C. Read (2nd edn., 1959), obviates the need for extended references to older works. See also D. Baker (ed.), *The Bibliography of the Reform ... relating to the United Kingdom ...* (Oxford, 1975). Most of the extant documents concerning Cromwell's policies are calendared in the 21 volumes of the *Letters and Papers of Henry VIII*, ed. J. S. Brewer, J. Gairdner and R. H. Brodie (1864–1929). R. B. Merriman, *The Life and Letters of Thomas Cromwell* (2 vols., 1902), prints in full a tiny proportion of these documents: those written by Cromwell himself. Merriman's introduction, especially the section on foreign policy, remains very valuable, yet he is curiously hostile and anxious to believe the worst. He even evolves an irresponsible fantasy to the effect that Cromwell may have poisoned Queen Katherine: Cromwell had, after all, spent time in Italy and she was in his way!

Of the earlier writers, almost the only one to emancipate himself from the prevalent spirit was P. Van Dyke in his *Renascence Portraits* (1906). The most important contributions to the study of Cromwell's ministry are those of Professor G. R. Elton. The articles are now collected in his *Studies in Tudor and Stuart Politics and Government* (2 vols., 1974). Also vital for the period are his recent books: *Policy and Police: the Enforcement of the Reformation in the Age of Thomas Cromwell* (1972), and *Reform and Renewal: Thomas Cromwell and the Common Ideal* (1973). For further sidelights see his *Star Chamber Stories* (1958). His article The Commons' Supplication of 1532 is criticised by J. P. Cooper in *English Historical Review*, lxxii (1957). An attractive recent account of both Wolsey and Cromwell is N. J. Williams, *The Cardinal and the Secretary* (1975). Excellent background reading, especially on the divorce, is afforded by J. J. Scarisbrick, *Henry*

VIII (1968). See also S. E. Lehmberg, *The Reformation Parliament* (1970). G. Mattingly, *Catherine of Aragon* (1950) is an able biography. A capacious selection of contemporary sources is in C. H. Williams, *English Historical Documents, 1485–1558* (1967).

B. Political Thought

On the political theory of the Cromwellian circle, two important books are available: W. G. Zeeveld, *Foundations of Tudor Policy* (1948), and F. L. Baumer, *The Early Tudor Theory of Kingship* (1940). Both contain valuable bibliographies. Professor Baumer has also written on Thomas Starkey and Marsiglio in *Politica*, ii (1936–7), and on St. German in *American Hist. Review*, xlii (1937). On social ideas, see also W. R. D. Jones, *The Tudor Commonwealth* (1970). On the Cromwell-Machiavelli problem, see Elton, 'The Political Creed of Thomas Cromwell', in his *Studies* (above), and T. M. Parker, 'Was Thomas Cromwell a Machiavellian?' in *Journal of Ecclesiastical Hist.*, i (1950). On Clement Armstrong, see S. T. Bindoff in *Economic History Review*, xiv (1944–5), and on Wilfrid Holme, A. G. Dickens in *Yorks. Archaeological Journal*, xxxix (1956). For the political writings of Stephen Gardiner, see P. Janelle, *Obedience in Church and State* (1930). There are valuable general accounts in J. W. Allen, *History of Political Thought in the Sixteenth Century* (1928), and in C. Morris, *Political Thought in England. Tyndale to Hooker* (1953).

C. The Monasteries and their Dissolution

The *Bibliography of British History* (above) has a section on this topic. All previous accounts were superseded by D. Knowles, *The Religious Orders in England*, vol. iii (1959). Other contributions are: G. W. O. Woodward, *Dissolution of the Monasteries* (1966), Joyce Youings, *The Dissolution of the Monasteries* (1971). *Visitations in the Diocese of Lincoln, 1517–1531*, ed. A. Hamilton Thompson (Lincoln Record Soc., xxxiii, xxxv, xxxvii, 1940–44–47); *Monastic Chancery Proceedings*, ed. J. S. Purvis (Yorks. Archaeol. Soc., Record Series, lxxxviii, 1934); *The Register or Chronicle of Butley Priory*, ed. A. G. Dickens (1951); E. M. Thompson, *The Carthusian Order in England* (1930); G. Baskerville, *English Monks and the* of monastic lands, see *Devon Monastic Lands: Calendar of Particulars for Grants*, ed. J. Youings (Devon and Cornwall Record Soc., new series, i, 1955). See also Dr Youings's article, 'The Terms of the Disposal of the Devon Monastic Lands', in Record Soc., new series, i). See also Dr Youings's article, 'The Terms of the Disposal of the Devon Monastic Lands', in *English Hist. Review*, lxix (1954). H. J. Habakkuk, 'The Market for Monastic Property, 1539–1603,' in *Economic History Review*, x (1958), deals with a variety of problems concerning the sale of the monastic lands. G. A. J. Hodgett's unpublished London M.A. thesis (1947). *The Dissolution of the Monasteries in Lincolnshire* has also much information on sales and speculation. Some of this is in his *Tudor Lincolnshire* (see below). On monastic pensions, see Baskerville (above); A. G. Dickens in *English Hist. Review*, lv (1940), and G. A. J. Hodgett in *Journal of Ecclesiastical History*, xiii (1962). A. Savine, *English Monasteries on the Eve of the Dissolution* (1909), remains indispensable for the economic side and for the *Valor Ecclesiasticus*.

D. The English Reformation

At present the 'standard' account of moderate length is A. G. Dickens, *The English Reformation* (1964; 4th edn., corrected, 1968). The best outline is T. M. Parker, *The English Reformation to 1558* (1950). P. Hughes, *The Reformation in England*, vol. i (1950), is capacious and scholarly; viewpoint, moderate Roman Catholic. The two volumes by H. Maynard Smith, *Pre-Reformation England* (1938) and *Henry VIII and the Reformation* (1948), are widely read and brightly written; viewpoint, clerical-Anglican. G. Constant, *The Reformation in England* (2 vols., 1934, 1942), is a selective partisan, but his references are valuable. The well-known general works on the Tudor period by S. T. Bindoff (1950), J. D. Mackie (1952) and G. R. Elton (1955) naturally contain much useful material on the Reformation and its periphery.

The following deal with special topics: J. F. Mozley, *Coverdale and his Bibles* (1953) is the best general account: viewpoint, strongly pro-Reformer. The same author's *William Tyndale* (1937) should be compared with the more impartial *William Tyndale* by C. H. Williams (1969). On *praemunire*, see W. T. Waugh in *English Hist. Review*, xxxvii

(1922); this is more lucidly summarized in *History, viii* (1923–4). Regarding the English Church on the eve of the Reformation, see A. Hamilton Thompson, *The English Clergy* (1947); Margaret Bowker, *The Secular Clergy of the Diocese of Lincoln, 1495–1520* (1967); P. Heath, *English Parish Clergy on the Eve of the Reformation* (1969). The crisis of 1514–15 is treated by A. Ogle, *The Tragedy of the Lollards' Tower* (1949) and by S. F. C. Milsom in *English Hist. Review*, lxxvi (1961). On leading doctrinal issues, see e.g., C. W. Dugmore, *The Mass and the English Reformers* (1958); P. Brooks, *Thomas Cranmer's Doctrine of the Eucharist* (1965); P. E. Hughes, *Theology of the English Reformers* (1965). On the early English Reformers, see E. G. Rupp, *The English Protestant Tradition* (1947); W. A. Clebsch, *England's Earliest Protestants* (1964). On the intellectual background, e.g. H. C. Porter, *Reformation and Reaction in Tudor Cambridge* (1958); J. K. McConica, *English Humanists and Renaissance Politics* (1965). On the Pardon of the Clergy, J. J. Scarisbrick, in *Cambridge Historical Journal*, xii (1956); on the Proclamations Act, E. R. Adair in *English Hist. Review*, xxxii (1917); on Treason by Words, I. D. Thornley in *ibid.* On the Henrician bishops, see L. B. Smith, *Tudor Prelates and Politics* (1953): among the best individual biographies are C. Sturge, *Cuthbert Tunstall* (1938) and J. Ridley, *Thomas Cranmer* (1962). For Robert Holgate, see *St. Anthony's Hall Publications*, no. viii (1955). W. Schenk, *Reginald Pole* (1950), is a sympathetic study.

E. Regional History

The social, economic and religious history of the Reformation, written on a regional basis, offers a promising field for research. A. L. Rowse, *Tudor Cornwall* (1941), is a learned and attractive survey of society, very informative on the Henrician Reformation. A. G. Dickens, *Lollards and Protestants in the Diocese of York* (1959), deals with the merging of these heresies from 1509 to 1558 and has a full account of Sir Francis Bigod. G. A. J. Hodgett, *Tudor Lincolnshire* (1975) is an excellent county-survey. On a distinctly Protestant area, see J. E. Oxley, *The Reformation in Essex* (1965). An outstanding regional study of another type is R. R. Reid, *The King's*

Council in the North (1921), which contains much else besides intitutional history. For recent assessments of the Pilgrimage of Grace, see A. G. Dickens in *Studies in Church History,* iv (1967); C. S. L. Davies in *Past and Present,* no. 41 (1968); M. E. James, 'Obedience and Dissent in Henrician England: the Lincolnshire Rebellion' in *Past and Present,* no. 48 (1970).

Index

192

194